Negotiation Genius On The Go Handbook

Proven Practices, Exercises and Routines for
Entrepreneur Mindset and Habits Biohacking

**Getting to Yes Is All That Matters When Deal's
Off Is Not an Option**

JEFFERSON KIARAN

CONTENTS

Introduction

Whether you are a pro-business person or just starting out, we all want new ways, methods, and knowledge that can make us a better and more successful entrepreneur.

What makes a better entrepreneur? What do you need to do to become legendary? What steps do you need to take to make yourself and your business sustainable? While these are all questions that do not have one answer, we have all heard the standard solutions to becoming a successful entrepreneur – how you need to take action, work hard, have passion, learn from mistakes and so on.

Yes, these are all essential points, tried and tested, which are the building blocks of a successful enterprise. However, this book endeavors to do much more. This book wants to give you deeper and more sustainable solutions to not only make you a better entrepreneur but one that stays ahead of the game and is extraordinary in every way.

Joining to a business meeting, presentation, or even worse, to a deal closing in poor psycho-physical conditions, will mean not to close on your terms at best, to blow up the deal at worst.

It doesn't matter **how** good you are but to be good **when** needed. All greatest managers are doomed to fail if these are the conditions. That's why cultivating high performance habits is the basis for those entrepreneurs, like you, always in a rush.

What will you gain?

- An understanding of how factors other than having stellar marketing and financial skills can make you a better entrepreneur.

- A more holistic and wholesome approach to becoming a successful entrepreneur.

- Cultivating a balanced healthy diet that enables you to enjoy eating even while on-the-go.

- Emphasis on mental health is an important factor towards success.

- Best practices, methods, and techniques to develop a lifestyle focused on a healthy mind and body to biohack your performance.

I hope you will enjoy this reading so to hear for your thoughts on Amazon.

Is this book for you?

This book is useful for many categories of entrepreneurs – from those who are in the fledgling stages to those who have been in the business for a long time – wanting to cultivate a higher level of thinking and operate on a different level in the business landscape.

Entrepreneurs who want more than just run-of-the-mill tactics and are looking for more profound ways to make an impact in their business, in their communities, and to their financial status will greatly benefit from the guidance herein. Because, this is for people who want to think differently – for those who want to live a better, happier, and more successful life.

This book is for those who want to develop the necessary psycho-physical skills to ensure that they are always ahead of the game, and for people looking to repair or reinvent habits that overlooked when we talk about successful entrepreneurship. It explores fixing and cultivating habits related to our mind and our body, which ultimately leads to a more sustainable business presence and a profound impact on the entrepreneur.

You know that there's no room for tiredness when on the go, there's no excuse due to overwork and that blurred mind is exactly what keeps you from achieving your goals.

Because, for people like you, getting to yes is all that matters when deal's off is not an option.

Are you ready to explore a greater and more robust approach in business?

Let's get started!

Typical problems in a business person's life

Before we move on to the amazing ways we can boost our entrepreneurship life from average to beast-mode, let's explore the issues commonly faced by entrepreneurs at any point of the entrepreneur life-cycle. These are common issues, so do not feel like you are a bad entrepreneur or that you should give up – problematic situations arise, but they are also easily remedied.

Time management

Time may be the biggest challenge faced by entrepreneurs because let's face it – you wear too many hats, and if only you had more time, you could accomplish more. It's either you have more time, or you learn how to manage your time better while lessening the time you take for more menial things. Identifying more productive ways to use your time is one of the golden goals of entrepreneurs.

Not knowing what to prioritize

As an entrepreneur, we are constantly trying to convince people that our product or service is worth having, and this also includes making our customers happy. When customers are happy, they will give you money in exchange for said product or service. The word 'no' is seldom uttered in the vocabulary of the entrepreneur, but in fact, is something that is said to ensure that goals are met. Each time you say no to something, it only means you can say yes to something more important and meaningful in your path to achieving your goals. How do you prioritize? Which goals are more important? That's something we will explore.

Unhealthy Addictions

Because of the lack of time, many entrepreneurs end up turning to unhealthy eating habits, which also lead to unhealthy addictions to certain types of food such as fast food, coffee, or even medication.

The idea of being successful means entrepreneurs often get swept up in emotions, which can also lead to unhealthy emotions and negativity, such as anxiety and stress. It is important to address these issues and learn how to navigate away from them.

Self-doubt

We may think that an entrepreneur's life is enviable, but that is far from the truth. Rarely do we see the blood, sweat, and tears that go into attaining success. Along the path to success, an entrepreneur also goes through self-doubt – especially when they have to keep trying various methods and ways to achieve their goals.

Being able to overcome self-doubt and instill a greater sense of confidence and self-esteem is a necessary trait for entrepreneurs. Having a good support system will help.

Importance of Maximizing Communication and Persuasion Skills in Business

So why is communication important in business? Communication is important in any setting, business or otherwise, but since this book is for entrepreneurs, let's take a quick look at the importance of good communication and persuasion skills in the business arena:

Clears Up Misunderstandings

When it comes to business, you want straightforward business negotiations. You do not want personal attacks, assumptions, or inaccurate information being passed around. If you are looking to branch out to overseas markets, good communication skills also include learning, respecting and understanding cultural differences and values. Effective communication is key to an entrepreneurs' success because it is the very essence that gets a product purchased, a store opened, a negotiation to go through, and the commencement of joint ventures.

Communication is an extremely effective tool to earn a client, close a deal, present your ideas, and gain trust. Business has always needed to ensure reliability to its clients and customers - this is the only way to prevent a business from crashing and burning. If customers trust your quality and trust your service, it is the best marketing tool you can have. One way to gain reliability and trust is to demonstrate accessibility.

Retention

Retention is an extremely important part of a business. Having retainer clients offers your business credibility which also earns the trust of many other potential clients because you offer them what they want, and you also listen to what they want and put their needs above all. This is a fundamental element for effective communication.

Common barriers

As an entrepreneur, you may run into communication gridlocks that can impact how much business you bring in and how much of that is retained. These barriers can be cultural differences, language, inconsistency, lack of transparency, or distrust. By communicating effectively, you earn this valuable trust and also retain your prospects and clients. It also reduces the noise from distorted perceptions made by your rivals.

SECTION 1: CULTIVATING GOOD EATING HABITS

***

The chapters in this section are dedicated to cultivating a healthy eating culture. One of the biggest reasons why entrepreneurs are addicted to unhealthy eating habits is because of the lack of time to cook and eat a well-balanced diet.

In this chapter, we explore the foundations of a healthy diet – and no, it's not all about Kale and broccoli – brain food that helps with clarity and focus, foods to eat when traveling or before a meeting, and easy and simple ways to cultivate a healthy eating plan.

This is the first, fundamental, aspect to be implemented in order to biohack your body and mind to ensure that essential psycho-physical conditions are always granted when on the move.

By the end of this section, you would have a better idea of how easy it is to eat right and how eating the right foods affect our mind and body, too. Your goal now is to revamp your eating habits by simply replacing the unhealthy with the healthy, little by little.

Chapter 1: Foundations of a Balanced, Healthy Diet

***

Being a business manager is by no means an easy feat. You will be spending a large part of your day attending meeting after meeting, either with your team members or customers. Let's not forget the commute time as well as traveling time that comes with the job. Your days can be so hectic at times that you can only afford around 3-4 hours of sleep before starting the sequence the next day. It is a well-known fact that time is very precious for any business people and they can't afford to waste a single second of the day doing something not productive.

More often than not, this kind of commitment starts to get in the way of being healthy. Since business people are always on the go, they start to pay less attention to the foods they consume daily. Hence, they make less than healthy choices when they choose their meal, and instead of consuming healthy options, they will usually resort to fast food type meals.

Making these unhealthy choices will have dire consequences; not only on a person's health but on their output and concentration at work.

It is extremely important that our bodies are kept well fed with proper nutrition to allow a busy individual with the energy they need to keep working at a fast pace. Therefore, it becomes pivotal that a balanced healthy diet is put in place to give the body the nourishment it needs.

What is the definition of a balanced and healthy diet? Nutrition experts define this as a diet that provides the body with the proper nutrition for the body to function satisfactorily.

A balanced and healthy diet will ensure that our organs and tissues get the right and proper nutrition for them to work properly. With a proper balanced and healthy diet, your body will be more adverse towards any infections, disease and will allow you to reduce fatigue and increase performance at work.

You should be consuming foods from sources such as whole grains, lean meats, nuts, fruits, and vegetables daily to ensure you are getting a well-balanced and healthy diet.

In the United States, four of the top 10 leading causes of deaths – heart disease, stroke, cancer, and diabetes – are attributed to lack of a proper balanced and healthy diet. To keep your body well-nourished to withstand the long working hours you will face daily, it's important to have the right type of foods in your diet. In a balanced diet, the foods that you should consume must be high in nutrients and vitamins but has to be low in fats and sugars.

Here are some examples of food groups that you can incorporate into your meals:

Protein

Protein is vital for the development of muscles in the body and as well as the function of the brain. Protein can be consumed from animals as well as plants. Chicken, fish, and beef are some of the sources of animal protein which are lean and low in fat. Trimming off excess fat and skin helps reduce the amount of fat and cholesterol that you consume. Opting for organic or grass-fed (beef and chicken) options is another option for you to consider when sourcing for your proteins. Plant-based protein is derived from sources such as almonds, walnuts, tofu, tempeh, lentils, and beans. Apart from being a good source of protein, these plant-based sources also provide other benefits such as fiber and other nutrients into your diet.

Dairy

Sources for dairy-based foods usually derive from cheese, milk, or yogurt. They provide calcium, vitamin D, and other important nutrients for the body. But it's important to keep in mind that these foods are also a major source of fats and it is best to consume these foods in small portions. Dairy can also be consumed from plant-based sources. These can be from items such as almond, soy, and flaxseed. Apart from having the same nutrients as animal-based dairy, they are fat-free and provide an excellent option to add to your diet.

Vegetables

No healthy diet is complete without the addition of vegetables – they are an excellent source of vitamins and minerals. The general recommendation is that you consume a variety of vegetables to obtain the various nutrients they have to offer. Some of the examples of vegetables you should be consuming are:

1. Broccoli

2. Kale

3. Carrots

4. Spinach

5. Collard Greens

6. Cabbage

Grains

A recent report by the USDA states that the consumption of refined white flour by Americans is higher than any other grain. This statistic is shocking, as white flour has very poor nutritional value compared to whole grains. Hence, it is advisable that when incorporating grains into your meals, you opt for whole grains, as they provide more nutrition compared to white flour – quinoa is an example of a healthy option to add some variety.

Fruits

Fruits can be added into your daily diet as snacks when you are on the go or between meals. Since fruits have high natural sugar content, they become a good alternative for those busy individuals looking to reduce refined sugar in their diet. Apart from that, fruits are a good source for carbohydrates and can be a good addition to your meals if you are trying to reduce carbs from your whole grain sources. Fruits can either be eaten whole or blended into a smoothie, so it's quite a versatile food group for those busy individuals.

Oils

If you are cooking your meals, use oils in moderation – if you are putting them into salads, go for low-fat options. Consume oils such as olive oil or coconut oil. It is also important to keep away from fried foods if you can only buy your meals during your workday.

Chapter 2: Brain Food – Food perfect for clarity and focus

***

Beyond the grocery store shelves filled with processed food, canned goods and brightly colored packaging there lies a whole other universe with healthy grains, beans, nuts, seeds, leafy vegetables and berries waiting for you to pick them up and place them in your grocery carts, to be taken back home and cooked into a scrumptious, satisfying, delicious and oh-so-healthy meal.

What's even more, eating the right foods can also help you improve mentally. Food has the immense ability to affect our moods, our mental clarity, as well as our ability to focus.

In this chapter, we will focus on (super) foods that you can consume to improve your memory, mood, focus, and clarity.

These foods will help if you are working on a project, about to present to stakeholders, need that extra mental boost, or simply need all the help you can get to focus on hitting your business milestones. Below is a list of superfoods from A-Z and its benefits for a healthy body and healthy mind.

FOOD ITEM	BENEFITS
Acai Berry	Native to South America, Acai berries are known for their amazing antioxidant content, twice more than blueberries. It also contains anthocyanins which help prevent heart diseases and improves cardiovascular health. Acai berries also **improve digestion** and slow down the process of aging.
Avocado	Avocados are an excellent source of monounsaturated fats. Monounsaturated fats help the body to improve cholesterol levels thus reducing the risk of heart-related diseases, and it is also known to **increase brain function**. It also contains vitamin E, a known antioxidant oil and vitamin B6 which benefits your skin! While nutritious, avocados are also high in calories.
Beets	This deep red superfood is high in betalain, which is an antioxidant that gives it is deep color. Beets help reduce cancer risks and other degenerative diseases. It also contains vitamins A, B & C that help **bolster the body's immune system** and produces collagen. It also contains potassium, to help the body's organ function. The fiber in beets also regulates the digestive system.
Bee Pollen	Collected from the bodies of the bees, bee pollen is high in vitamins, carbohydrates, and lipids. It helps with asthma, **combats fatigue,** reduces allergic reactions and also increases your body's **energy levels.**
Blueberries	The fact that blueberries are high in antioxidants make it perfect in slowing the aging process, and it also fights free radicals that cause cancer and Alzheimer's. It is also an effective antidepressant that can **help stabilize mood swings.**
Chia Seeds	Chia seeds, small as they come, are packed with an array of vitamins and minerals such as iron, calcium,

	magnesium, and potassium. Chia seeds are so versatile that you can include them in salads and smoothies, yogurt and puddings. It also absorbs up to 10 times of weight in water, which is why eating them in the morning makes you **stay hydrated and full longer, thus improving the body's endurance.**
Cacao	Cacao, in its raw and unadulterated form, is full of health benefits so if you have cacao, having with a raw dessert is the best way. Cacao, another South American origin is rich in antioxidants and lipids. It **aids in depression,** increases cardiovascular health and reduces the effects of free radicals.
Dates	Dates are a great substitute for butter and sugar when it comes to baking. That's why vegans love it! They have very high fiber content which aids in heart health and digestive system. It also has selenium and magnesium.
Eggs	Yes, eggs have so many benefits plus they're yummy too! Eggs contain the right amount of protein and omega-3 fatty acids which aid in bodily functions and heart health too. They also contain antioxidants called lutein and zeaxanthin which protects our eyes from the light and free radicals and slows down eye degeneration due to age. Some say yolks are bad news because of their high cholesterol content but yolks contain choline, which is a vitamin B component that **aids in brain function.**
Flax seeds	Flax seeds have amazingly high fiber content and the omega 3 in the seeds help lower cholesterol levels. It also promotes bone health and is said to aid in breast cancer prevention. You can add the seeds either whole or ground into oatmeal, granola, salads and even baked goods.
Grapes	Grapes are full of the goodness of beta-carotene and vitamins C & K. This fruit also contains antioxidants that help to **eliminate free radicals in the body that can cause cellular damage**. It also contains

	a component that contains resveratrol that purportedly reduces LDL cholesterol in the blood as well as inhibits cancer cell growth. Grapes are also **great to treat cognitive impairment.**
Goji Berries	Goji berries have one of the highest concentrations of protein, and it contains amino acids essential to the body, and a healthy dose of vitamin A. One tablespoon of goji berries has only 18 calories which make them a great snack option. Goji berries are a favorite for pre-workout snacks as they **increase energy levels and improve athletic performance.** Consumption of goji berries also helps the mind to **stay focused and sharp.**
Ginger	Ginger is one of the favorite spices in Asia and for good reason. It is used in many herbal concoctions and alternative medicine as it contains high-powered benefits that can reduce inflammation and bellyaches, nausea, diarrhea and clear up respiratory infections and other common ailments. Ginger mixed with honey and tea is an excellent way to heal sinuses and asthma.
Hemp	Hemp has essential fatty acids and protein that help in coronary heart disease as well as combating cancer and certain symptoms of depression. They also have high amounts of magnesium, iron and zinc and are great for fighting allergies and it is also used to **treat attention deficit disorder.**
Inca Berries	Apart from Gogi, quinoa and acai, here's another superfood from South America. Inca berries are crazy high with vitamins A, C, iron, niacin and phosphorous. High in fiber and protein also make it great for salads and post-workout meals.
Jalapeno Peppers	The main compound found in Jalapenos is called capsaicin, which is credited for speeding up metabolism and also can suppress appetites. Capsaicin also increases fat oxidation which **enables**

	the body to use fat as fuel more effectively.
Kiwi	Kiwi contains high amounts of vitamin C, even more than oranges. A great source of folate, which contributes to overall health. Studies have shown that kiwi can also reduce the risk of colon cancer and heart diseases.
Lemon	Lemon and other citrus fruits are jam-packed with vitamin C, which is essential to the production of collagen that keeps bones healthy and strong, tendons and ligaments well lubricated. Lemons can be used for beauty regimens and also has skin and teeth whitening properties.
Milk	Milk or more specifically chocolate milk has some serious post-workout health benefits. It is the quintessential energy drink that has the right balance of carbohydrates and protein. Chocolate milk **improves performance and recovery periods.** It also leads to improved body composition.
Nuts	Nuts, apart from being irresistibly delicious and a great additional to various deserts, it also contains unsaturated fats that are essential for the body's growth. Different nuts can help lower blood pressure and body fat. It is also a great source of protein which makes it a good post-workout snack. While they may be high in calories, they also are nutrient dense.
Oats	Oats are an excellent source of fiber and minerals. They help lower blood cholesterol and aids in digestion as well as improve metabolism. It is always good to make your oatmeal as opposed to buying the pre-made, instant variety in the store so that you cut out on any additives and unnecessary sugar.
Pumpkin	Pumpkins are so versatile, and they are delicious in salads and desserts, breakfast puddings and roasts. Pumpkin is also another food item rich in antioxidants and vitamins such as beta-carotene, fiber as well as Vitamin K, which is great to promote

	eye health and reduce cancer risks. Pumpkin seeds are equally healthy as they are packed with protein, magnesium, potassium, and zinc.
Pistachio	Pistachio is cholesterol free and high in fiber and protein. These nuts have amazing amounts of potassium and are great to eat to fill your stomach. It helps keep LDL cholesterol low while having high antioxidants. Pistachios are great for weight management and for heart health.
Quinoa	This couscous lookalike is related to leafy vegetables like Swiss chard and Kale. Quinoa has nine essential amino acids that our body cannot produce naturally.
Radish	This crunchy root vegetable can be found in white usually called daikon and red. Certain compounds found in radishes help fight the growth of cancerous cells, especially breast cancer. Radishes also contain anthocyanins which aid in muscle recovery after a tough workout.
Salmon	Salmon is the only fish that swims against the currents which are why they are on the superfood list! They have amazing benefits and contain healthy omega-3 fatty acids that can reduce the risk of cardiovascular diseases. Salmon's Omega-3s also benefit the skin by protecting it from UV damage.
Tea	Tea is a well known ancient tonic that is ideal for plenty of things and has so many health benefits. It boosts endurance; it reduces the risk of heart issues, it can reduce the risks of cancer, it hydrates the body, **it prevents damage from free radicals, and it also detoxifies.**
Watermelon	Watermelons are packed with water and have only 48 calories. This refreshing fruit is perfect for a healthy snack and a low sugar drink. It is high in vitamins A and C and has amino acid citrulline. Watermelons are also a great source of lycopene which has the essential carotenoid usually found in tomatoes. Carotenoid

	protects the body from UV rays and certain forms of cancer.
Yams	This tuber has very low glycemic index and can be consumed in high amounts without affecting your blood sugar levels. They are a great source of energy and also fiber, vitamin B6, potassium, and manganese.
Zucchini	Zucchini, a stable in most grocery cards can be used in both savory and sweet dishes. It is packed with vitamins B6 and C, and also potassium, manganese, and folate. Zucchini is used in many salads as it is low in calories and high in water content making salads a refreshing summer treat.

Chapter 3: Incorporating Superfoods into your Diet

*****

You've probably had a combination of the superfoods listed in the previous chapter in some of the cuisines and meals throughout your life. However, most people tend to follow an unhealthy diet which reduces the number of superfoods they consume, or their diet consists of a select few ingredients – in other words, there is no variety. Variety is vital for everyone. A combination of protein, carbohydrates, vegetables, nuts, grains, beans, and dairy is essential for a healthy body.

But if your diet usually consists of burgers and fries, fast food, soda drinks and fried foods, the likelihood of you eating anything that isn't brown or fried isn't very high. A large number of people eat too many of the wrong foods simply because they have not developed a taste for nutritional food, aren't aware of the consequences of unhealthy food, or just couldn't be bothered to alter their diet.

Old habits are hard to break – on the other hand, it isn't entirely impossible.

If you are planning on revamping your diet and would like to eat the rainbow so to speak, then there are several ways that you can sneak in these superfoods to up the ante of your diet game.

Whatever diet you choose or the foods you want to consume, the general rule is to have loads of fruits, vegetables, nuts, beans, dairy, and omega 3- fatty acid rich foods. Even if you do consume a good mix, the challenge is to include more of these amazingly nutritious foods into your daily diet. The bigger challenge is that not many people aren't big fans of superfoods' taste or texture.

However, according to Evelyn Tribole, co-author of the *Stealth Health: How to Sneak Nutrition Painlessly Into Your Diet*, working power foods into your diet is all about eating the right recipes. Evelyn recommends looking into the favorite foods you eat or the kind of food that you eat regularly and figuring out how to add in some of these superfoods.

For example, if you love eating tuna casseroles or fish patties, you can make a smart substitute by opting for salmon as a seafood choice rather than tuna, cod, or mackerel.

Another example is sneaking in flax seed. It seems pretty hard to think of how to include something that seems so non-versatile such as flax seeds, but you can incorporate it into your granola for your morning breakfast or even muffins, soups and of course salads.

Conquering Food Biases

Our tastes buds evolve as time passes. Think of how you loved sweet things when you were a kid. The urge to have very sweet food may not be as apparent when you get into adulthood. Also, predetermined ideas of food can cause people not to try these foods before they even taste it.

For example, when you were younger, you probably hated broccoli because of the way it was prepared. But certain foods can taste amazing if you cook them differently.

Consider giving broccoli a chance by changing the visual presentation of the dish. You can puree broccoli if you don't like the way it is. You can even roast, dice it, and shred it even. The objective is to change the appearance of your least favorite food, so you can improve the odds of you eating it by changing its appearance or texture.

One Step at a Time

If you want to make a healthy change and start eating more superfoods, remember not to overdo it. The problem everyone makes when starting something new, whether eating healthily, exercising, attempting a new habit or even learning a new skill, is starting strong and hard but not having the momentum to get through. So even with changing your dietary habits, remember you do not have to eat all superfoods at one go or all the time.

The idea is to start small and make dietary tweaks one at a time till it becomes a habit.

David Katz, MD says "Pick three things you can do each day, do it consistently, and it will become a habit," says Katz, co-author of the book *Stealth Health: How to Sneak Age-Defying, Disease-Fighting Habits into Your Life without Really Trying*. "It is the routines and habits that integrate good health into your lifestyle that will result in health and wellness."

One of the steps to take is substituting certain non-healthy items with smart alternatives such as choosing whole grains over refined grains. David Katz suggests to start with easy replacing, so the benefits encourage you to create other substitutions and other changes.

Also, expanding your tastes buds is a good idea. Sometimes, we may not be used to a certain food item such as chia seeds or bee pollen, but keep trying to consume it. It may take some time before you add these foods to your favorite food list.

Research has shown that it takes up to 8 or 9 times for anyone to get used to eating a particular type of food before their eating preference is established.

Nutrition Tips from Evelyn Tribble and David Katz

Here are 15 tips to help you sneak in some superfood into your diet:

1- BLEND IT

Blending smoothies is an excellent idea to get those lesser eaten fruits and vegetables into your stomach. Smoothies are great for a snack, for breakfast and even for pre or post- workout meals.

2- TOP IT

Using foods like tomatoes, leafy greens, nuts and even chia seeds as toppings for sandwiches and salads is an extremely easy way to upgrade your meal from average to healthy. Crunchy whole-grain cereal or flavorful granola is elevated into an amazing, nutrition dense breakfast with the addition of yogurt. Adding a bagful of spinach under your pizza toppings is a great way of adding greens to your meal.

3- PUREE IT

Pureeing food items is a great way of altering the texture, so it is much easier to eat. Pureed roasted vegetables make for a satisfying sauce as a side or even for dipping with chicken or fish meals. Pureed cauliflower is delicious as a topping for burgers. Pureed avocado becomes a great complement for salads.

4- STIR IT

In Asian cuisine, vegetables are shredded before being added to fried rice, fried noodles, ramen, or broth. Soups, stews, meatloaf, omelets, and quiches are ideal recipes where carrots, cucumbers, beets, garlic, avocado, and leafy greens are added without compromising taste.

5- USE THIS NOT THAT

Substitute rice for cauliflower rice. Substitute dairy milk for almond milk in baking. Instead of beef or chicken, substitute it for tempeh. Substitute ricotta cheese with blended tofu, honey with agave syrup, and butter with olive oil. The options are endless.

6- BAKE IT

Everyone loves the smell coming out from the oven. You can upgrade bread and muffins to a healthy option by adding bananas, blueberries, pumpkin, zucchini, carrots, and walnuts.

7- ROAST, GRILL OR BROIL IT

Fruits and vegetables don't have to be eaten fresh all the time. Some roasting, grilling, and broiling elevates the subtle flavors of a variety of vegetable and fruits. For example, oven-dried cherry tomatoes give out an earthy flavor to any dish. Grilled jalapeno adds a rustic touch to any burger, and grilled Portobello mushrooms are so good you can eat them on their own.

8- DIP IT

Make amazing dips with fruits such as an orange cream dip which is refreshing and delicious. A raspberry fruit dip is great as an addition to an afternoon tea spread. A coconut cream dip is a welcome on a hot summer afternoon.

9- EAT RAW

Of course, eating things raw is probably the easiest way to eat things. If you do not have time to make stuff, then cut them up and nibble it away. Celery on its own is great and can be eaten with minimal attention. Eat raw cucumbers, jicama, or even a handful of goji and blueberries as a snack – it's a great way to increase your superfood intake by eating raw.

10- BUY PRE-CUT

Sometimes, if you are lazy, purchasing pre-cut vegetables and fruits will increase the chances of you eating them. Also, purchase vegetable or fruit drinks such as cold pressed pomegranate or cold pressed celery and cucumber juice.

11- DISGUISE IT

Shredding things like lemon or spiraling zucchini and cucumber to add it into your pasta is an excellent disguise method.

12- SPICE IT

Herbs, spices, and vinegar are essential to the body and to flavor food when cooking. Make your healthy salads and soups come alive but simply adding oregano, basil, rosemary, and thyme. Doing this can take a boring meal to a top-notch restaurant level cuisine.

13- EXPERIMENT

Sometimes, changing the way you cook things will make you look forward to cooking and eating it more often. For example, eggplant is a great vegetable to cook Asian by lightly sautéing it and just added garlic and soy sauce to create an easy yet delicious vegetable dish. Salmon is super delicious cooked with teriyaki sauce. Yam is always cooked as a steamed cake in Chinese cuisine. Turmeric, chilies, onions are a staple in Indian cooking.

14- BE ADVENTUROUS

Cooking on your own is a great way to pique interest and try new things in your kitchen. If it doesn't turn out the way you want, learn from it and attempt to do it again. Start with simple dishes and work your way up by improving your cooking techniques and venturing outside your comfort zone. Try different cuisines and continue finding ways to add in superfoods to your culinary adventure.

15- SEE HOW PROFESSIONALS PREPARE

With the multitude of cooking videos available online, it is easy to figure out the steps used to prep and cook a protein like fish, chicken, or beef. Watching how chefs and nutritional experts reinvent items like vegetables, nuts, and seeds is an excellent eye-opener.

Chapter 4: Cultivating a Regulated, Healthy Eating Routine

***

With most of your time spent in the office attending meeting after meeting, maintaining healthy eating habits became an uphill battle. Hence, cultivating a healthy eating plan is important to maintain focus and energy level that you will need throughout the day. Here are some tips and options that you can employ into your busy schedules that will set you on the road for having a healthy eating routine.

Don't skip breakfast

It's been repeated too many times till it's become a sort of a cliché. Breakfast is the most important meal of the day. Breakfast gives you the jumpstart you need to get your busy day going. However, the challenge most business people have is preparing a healthy breakfast due to their jam-packed schedule first thing in the morning. So often you'll find yourself grabbing cereal or pastries loaded with sugars, making them less of an ideal option as a healthy meal. For the busy person, here are some tips on having healthier choices for breakfast that you can have while on the go:

Scrambled Eggs: No fuss here. Just toss some eggs with any leftover veggies. Throw in some minced chicken or leftover bacon bits for that extra protein. Don't forget to season it with a bit of salt and pepper while you're at it. Just make sure you use olive oil or coconut oil as a healthier alternative.

Fruit Smoothies: You can opt for fruits such as bananas, watermelon, or even berries. Throw in some chia seeds and kale for added nutrient and blend this all together with either low-fat milk, almond milk, or even coconut milk and you got a delicious and nutritious breakfast that you can consume while commuting from home to work.

Drink plenty of water

Nutrition experts and medical professionals have always advised that we need to drink at least eight 8-ounce glasses of water every day. This rule usually applies for a normal day, but if required, drink a bit more.

If you're going to be stuck in the office the whole day, try to make it a habit of having a glass of water for every hour that you are in the office. Keeping yourself well hydrated will ensure your organs are working at their optimum level and you're performing well at work each day. You can either opt to keep a bottle of water at your desk or take a few trips to office "watering hole" to get some additional exercise clocked in while you're at it.

When eating out, choose healthier options

As a business person, you'll constantly find yourself having to treat others or having lunch meetings. Instead of going for that burger or steak, try ordering something off the menu that is healthier. Instead of fried foods, go for grilled instead. Order a salad or veggies instead of those french fries or onion rings. Ditch the soda and go for plain water or worst case, diet coke. Green tea can also be an option. If you find yourself not being able to get anything healthy off the menu, then discipline yourself to limit the amount of food that you consume.

Meal prep

The best way to ensure you are eating healthy is to prepare your meals in advance to save precious time in the mornings. You can either choose to prepare an entire weeks worth of meals in advance, but we suggest you prep for at least three or four days to keep your food fresh. If you want your meals to be super fresh then just prep them the night before. It's best to invest in good plastic containers in which you can store your meals. You can prep your meals on a Sunday night just before going to bed and keep them refrigerated. Another advantage of meal prep that is overlooked is that it will be much kinder to your pocket. Since you're prepping the similar meals in advance, you not only save time but money as well since you will be buying the same ingredients.

Limit the alcohol intake

A large and important part of business is networking. Having a large and influential network is key to the success of any business. Hence, many business people will want to attend as many networking events in hopes of expanding their business. More often than not, this kind of networking activities takes place with alcohol. So when you're planning to start on this new healthy eating routine, consuming alcohol even in moderation may be the last thing you need right now to add on unwanted calories. If you can't avoid alcohol completely at a function, don't sweat it, as long as you are practicing the other tips that we have discussed earlier, you should be in the clear. Just have drinks in moderation and try to limit your nights out as you deemed fit. It is important to be flexible when maintaining a healthy diet. One bad meal won't derail your efforts.

Utilizing food delivery apps

Time is an essential part of a business people's lives – after all, time is money. They can't waste a precious minute doing something non-productive, and as mentioned above, they tend to neglect the importance of eating healthy. With the latest advances in mobile phone technology and the introduction of food delivery apps, busy people get food without needing to leave the office. With just a few quick steps, healthy foods from nearby shops are delivered, without having to interrupt a busy workday. Apart from purchasing food online, some apps also allow groceries to be bought and delivered to a residence at a convenient time for the customer. The only drawback for these apps is that there are some delivery charges when using their services, but with such a busy lifestyle, the time saved is worth its weight in gold.

Chapter 5: Foods to Avoid Before a Meeting, Presentation or Business Travel

***

A large part of a business person's scope of work is traveling - whether it is by air or land (or in some cases by sea). And for many of us, we may be making two or three flights within a day to get from one city to another.

Hence making these trips pleasurable is of the utmost importance, not only to get ready for our next meeting but also to use the downtime to get some work done. So the last thing you need is to feel ill while traveling because you consumed the wrong type of food before or during your commute.

Here are some foods to avoid to prevent this:

Meat and Egg Products

For long haul flights, best to skip protein based foods that tend to create hydrogen sulfide gas. It takes three to four hours to produce this gas so if your flight or drive is longer than an hour or two, best to avoid these foods.

Nuts

When nuts are digested in our body, they create intestinal gas. Some common types of nuts that have this effect are almonds, cashews, and pistachios. Their fibers are fermented in our body's digestive system and create these intestinal gases. It ends up causing bloating, and the effect tends to get worse when you are in a pressurized cabin of an aircraft.

Dried Fruit

Dried fruit while having a high content of sugar and calories, also create intestinal gases. If eaten in high quantities, they tend to add a lot of sorbitol and fiber to our gut, which draws out water creating high amounts of intestinal gases.

Gum and Mints

The last thing you need while on a train or a flight is having bloating or diarrhea. So stay away from snacks that are high in sugar alcohols like xylitol, mannitol, and sorbitol.

Hummus

Hummus is another gas inducing food that you want to avoid to prevent bloating. This also includes dried beans, soybeans, lentils, edamame, and bean dips.

Granola Bars

Granola bars that contain chicory root is another no-no. Chicory root is a food that can induce bloating because it contains fermented fibers. So make sure to check the label before you buy them.

Potato Chips

Acid reflux, bloating, and swelling in the hands and feet are some of the symptoms you can expect to have if you are consuming potato chips in large amounts during your travels. The snacks are high in fat and salt and provide little or no nutrition at all. Having a considerable amount of salt can induce water retention that promotes bloating. You might also want to stay clear of the pretzels and peanuts that are often offered as snacks on flights.

In preparing for a presentation, don't think that sipping on some alcohol is going to calm your nerves. Would you be comfortable if your pilot downs a couple of pints just before take-off because he or she is feeling nervous? I didn't think so. It won't help you be a better presenter since alcohol is shown to have an adverse effect on your memory.

When you are nervous, you're already going to have problems remembering your slides and notes, and adding alcohol into the mix won't do you any good. Alcohol will also inhibit your thinking process, concentration, and speech pattern, which are all critical for an excellent presentation. And don't forget, drinking alcohol will affect your breath. So best to stay away from that practice if you don't want to turn off your audience. A celebratory drink afterward is a better idea.

Apart from that, here are other foods to stay away from before a presentation:

- Dairy - Will build up mucus in your throat. Don't consume milk, ice cream, cheese and yogurt.

- Orange Juice - Will cause thickening of saliva.

- Fatty Foods - Will take time to digest. Hamburger, fries, pizza and even caffeinated drinks.

- Sodas - These drinks may induce gas and bloat. Also, try to avoid cruciferous vegetables such as broccoli and cauliflower to prevent this from happening.

- Water - Seem trivial, right? But go easy on the liquid as you don't want to be running to the restroom in the middle of your presentation.

When choosing catering food for a meeting, it is essential to consider what type of food you are going to order and how it will work best for your office. Here are some foods you want to avoid ordering and having before or during a meeting:

Garlic and Onion

Your business meetings are going to revolve around a lot of discussions with either your peers, subordinates, or customers. So let's not give them an unpleasant experience with your breath. Bad breath is one of the worse things to deal with when communicating with someone. So stay away from any food that contains garlic or onions.

Spicy Foods

Not everyone can agree to a curry based cuisine, so it's best not to have any if it isn't a staple part of your diet. Having a bowl of super-hot curry might sound tasty, but it could leave you red-faced and gasping for air and water.

Spaghetti

No one likes a suit tainted with sauce stains before a meeting - not a good first impression. Hence, best to be safe and leave this meal for when you're back home and able to be messy.

Ribs and Wings

These are great for after-work snacks with drinks but never before a formal meeting. It is just too messy. Anything that requires you to wear a bib is best left for after exiting the boardroom.

Chapter 6: Meal Prep for the Busy Entrepreneur

***

When it comes to weight loss, getting leaner and fitter, or eliminating body fat - we look at food as a tool to change and manipulate our bodies.

In this process, we miss the basic idea of food. Our connection to food is to nourish the body, and when you feed the body the right way, it not only affects your waistline, it also affects you psychologically and emotionally.

The psychology of eating is all about connecting our emotional and mental state to the whole eating experience. When we nourish and fuel our bodies; we nourish our minds and souls.

When we talk about diet, it's always about manipulating our body or putting it through starvation mode. However, the term diet can simply mean a way of life.

Food should make us feel good and what we eat directly affects how we feel. If it tastes great and nourishes our bodies at the same time- bonus points! Not having a pleasant experience with food ultimately leads to negative feelings.

Meal preparation is a way of life, as well. It is a form of diet that looks at healthy and wholesome home-cooked meals and also learning how to portion control.

The Psychology of Meal Prepping

Meal prepping teaches us to make healthier and mindful decisions with our food choices over time, thus improving our relationship with food. Meal prepping also teaches us to control our compulsive eating and binging- it enables us to take charge of our appetite.

By picking and choosing your food ingredients in the market, coming home and cutting, peeling, chopping and dicing and then moving on to sautéing, cooking, roasting, steaming and so on- you have put in plenty of effort into making your food.

These steps have made you take charge of your appetite through food preparation. While it may seem like a daunting task at first and granted, there could be plenty of times that things have gone wrong, you ultimately made a meal.

Taking charge and cooking something makes people feel calm and increases the alertness to the foods that you eat.

Meal prepping changes plenty of deep-seated and unhealthy relationships with food and promotes:

- Better body movement.

- Positive body image.

- Positive relationships with food.

- Increased alertness and energy levels.

- Makes eating healthy not so challenging.

What aspects influence our eating behaviors?

Experts believe many aspects of life can influence our feelings and relationships with food and our eating behaviors.

These factors include:

- Cultural.

- Evolutionary.

- Social.

- Family.

- Individual.

- Economic status.

- Psychological.

Many of us use food as a coping mechanism in facing the emotions we go through, such as boredom, stress, anxiety, and depression. This is great for short term mood alleviation, but as it goes on, this leads to guilt and regret. We end up eating more to suppress these emotions, leading to even more negative emotions. Ultimately, our self-image suffers as we start gaining weight.

What role does psychology play in meal planning?

Psychology is a behavioral science that looks into how and why people act as they do. For people wanting to lose weight or become leaner, psychology studies:

- Behavior - Identifies a person's eating patterns and behaviors and finds a way to change them.

- Cognition (thinking) - Therapy is conducted to identify self-defeating thinking patterns that contribute to weight management and eating problems.

By getting ourselves involved with meal preparation, we pay more attention to our food and savor what we eat much more than if it was purchased off the rack or cooked in a restaurant. Eating these foods is easy and tempting, but the excitement fades once we are full and satiated.

Meal prepping allows us to be more grateful, mindful, and appreciative of what goes into our mouths and the source of where it came from.

How Eating Right and Meal Prepping Makes You A Better Entrepreneur

You may not expect it, but eating right and meal prepping can benefit your abilities as an entrepreneur. Here are some healthy habits that well-known entrepreneurs practice, which you may feel inspired to follow as well:

Seth Godin, bestselling author and blogger -He does the same thing for breakfast every day- a smoothie made from frozen bananas, almond milk, hemp powder, walnuts and dried plums. While you may not have to eat the same thing every morning, it pays to have a routine. If you are short of time, meal prep your smoothie ingredients ahead of time and get yourself a personal blender that enables you to juice on the go.

Victoria Beckham, Fashion Designer, Entrepreneur, Model, Singer -She is an ardent follower of the Alkaline diet. This diet promises to increase energy levels, improve memory as well as reduce heart diseases, bloating, and insomnia. She usually starts her day with a glass of hot water with lemon juice to kickstart the alkaline levels and follows through with eating mostly raw food and eliminating refined sugar.

Martha Stewart, businessperson, retailer, writer and TV personality -With a name that needs no introduction, Martha, although 76, looks like she's in her 50s. Her diet plan consists of a green juice every single morning, considerable dose of organic vegetables, and preference towards a fish based diet.

Sundar Pichai, CEO of Google -Sundar is a vegetarian who usually starts his day with toast, an omelette for protein, and tea.

Mark Cuban, host of Shark Tank and billionaire -Commits to at least an hour of cardiovascular exercise every day. He drinks smoothies and eats yogurt as part of his pre and post workout meals.

Some of the most apparent benefits to meal prepping:

You will be investing in your health

Meal prepping allows you to plan on what you'll be eating throughout the week. People who meal prep have a high chance of eating cleaner and healthier, as compared to those who do not. When you have healthy food options readily available, you are less likely to go after something bad for you.

You will have better willpower

Meal prepping gets you into a routine, and over time, you'll find yourself eating healthy more consistently. The more you meal prep breakfast, lunch, dinner, and snacks, the more you'll realize that you have fewer cravings. It also makes it easier for you to prevent any binge eating.

It will reduce stress

Walking about aimlessly in a grocery store is a cause for anxiety. Not knowing what to eat daily is also a cause for stress. Stress can affect your mind and body in various ways. It can have an adverse effect on your digestive system for starters, which will then lead to disruptive sleeping patterns and affect your immune system. Meal prepping will stop you from saying 'What's for lunch or What's for Dinner.' Instead, you'll probably reach out to whatever packed food is in your fridge, heat it, and eat it. It makes more time for you and your family, you have more time to relax, especially on weekdays, and you will have good food to eat.

You will also save time

You only need to invest a certain amount of time at the beginning of the week to plan, prep, cook, and pack. After that, you save time away from the kitchen, and the only time you need to be in the kitchen is to heat your food. You don't need to figure out what to cook every day, which leads to last minute and frequent trips to the store each time you want to cook.

SECTION 2: CULTIVATING GOOD PHYSICAL HABITS

***

Now that we've covered the essential bits of eating right, it's time to look into what we do to care for ourselves physically. A focused and clear mind comes with eating right and staying active. What you eat needs to be accompanied by cultivating a habit of exercise, sleeping for the right number of hours, having a healthy morning routine, and meditating.

That's what makes the difference when it comes to entrepreneur's performance allowing him to over-perform during crucial conversations.

We will look at exercise routines that are perfect for travelling – being this an essential aspect of an entrepreneur's life – as well as on creating a healthy routines to overclock entrepreneur's performances.

Once you finish this chapter, you should look into your current habits and start changing them to incorporate more healthy practices into your daily life. You'd be surprised how the smallest tweaks can make the most significant impact toward becoming a fantastic entrepreneur.

Chapter 7: Benefits of Daily Exercise

***

It is a known fact that regular exercise can protect your health and help you maintain an ideal body weight in the long run. But did you know that it can also yield additional benefits for the busy professional such as yourself? Studies have shown that regular exercise releases hormones to boost your mood, reduce stress, helps you sleep better at night, and - if performed in the mornings - help jump-start your day. In the end, exercise helps to boost productivity at work and ultimately boost the success of your business. Here are some examples of how regular exercise can help not only improve your health but your professional career as well:

Improve Your Network

Apart from networking functions, working out at the gym, or any sports related activity can provide an opportunity to meet individuals, which can help strengthen and widen your existing business relationships. A lot of individuals resort to taking up golf as one avenue to broaden their circle, but other sports also offer the same kind of opportunities. Even the gym provides the same possibility as you tend to meet people with similar interest and background as you. Exercising with others allows you to show your personality and communicate in a way that is different than if you had met in the boardroom.

Goal Setting and Determination

When you start exercising or picking up a new sport, try to always set goals to achieve. The training you put into these goals, such as completing a marathon, can help business professionals use that same determination and drive to pursue the challenges and objectives in the boardroom.

Increase Your Confidence

Every time you hit the gym and accomplish a goal that you set for that workout, you begin to feel good about yourself. This accomplishment of having a great workout, can translate into every area in your life and improve your confidence level throughout the day. Having confidence makes you feel great about everything you set yourself up to do.

Improve Creativity and Thinking Skills

Studies have shown that exercise benefits not only the physical part of your body, but also the mental part. Cardio exercise not only improves aerobic capabilities of an individual but improves their cognitive functions as well. The increase in blood flow to the brain has shown to be the leading cause of this increase.

Reduces Stress

When we are stressed, we notice that we are unable to act and think properly; thus, we end up making a lot of not-so-good decisions at work. Exercising helps us battle this stress by releasing endorphins when we induce our bodies through physical activities. These endorphins give us a natural high and allow us to approach our day with a calmer mindset.

Increase Energy Levels

Working day in and day out can lead to an increase in fatigue levels for an individual. If you don't fight this, you end up going to work with low energy levels that will inhibit your performance. In a study done on the effect of exercise on an individual's energy levels, it was shown that performing exercises daily helped them to increase their energy levels by 20 percent - while it also helped to reduce their fatigue levels by 65 percent.

Exercising regularly not only helps you to be awake throughout the entire day, it also enables you to get better sleep at night. We have gone through some of the crucial points of why exercising is both physically and mentally important to a busy professional like yourself. If you have not exercised before or have trouble getting into a routine, it can be a daunting task to reap those benefits that we spoke off earlier. So, the best thing we need to do to build a routine out of exercising is to make a plan.

Here are steps that we can take:

Goal Setting

Determine the individual goals that you want to achieve. It can be anything from reducing your weight to picking up a new sport. Whatever the reason, be sure to write it down and focus on it.

Choosing Your Workout Times

Choose a time in the day that you feel you can focus and complete your workouts. Many enjoy working out first thing in the morning, while others enjoy evening workouts - you can sneak in an exercise during lunch time if your office has a gym as well. But ultimately, you have to decide what is best for you, by choosing a routine that you will most likely stick to, based on your busy schedule. One of the most important things to get in the habit of is listening to your body. If you are still sore from your previous workout, or you are feeling tired, it's best to skip the workout for that day and start again when you feel better.

Choosing an Exercise

Once you have set your goals and workout time, it is time to choose what workout you want to do. This can be as simple as going for a jog or walk. Swimming is another popular exercise that is easy and convenient to do. Joining a local gym and signing up for their aerobic or yoga classes also is a popular choice amongst busy professionals. How about hitting those weights? Don't know where to start? Get a personal trainer to help you through the basic movements. The most important criteria to remember is to select an activity, whether it be a solo or a group activity, that you are likely to stick to in the long run and make part of your daily routine.

Learn To Have Fun

The one final thing that you will need to know once you have covered all of the other aspects above is to have fun with the exercise you are doing. Ensure that the activity that you have chosen doesn't make you feel bored. Exercise should be fun, and when you keep things energized, you're less likely to give up. So for this, try to join a class or get a workout partner push you and keep you occupied.

Chapter 8: Meditation to relieve stress and fatigue

***

It is a universal truth that meditation is a crucial treatment in stress management.

A hectic, non-stop, and on the go lifestyle seems to be the norm for many these days - just another example of how our lives have changed over time. We sometimes get so busy that we completely forget to take care of ourselves, and because of that, our health has paid the price. The result of poor health is stress and anxiety.

The reason that so many struggle to find calmness is because they have lost their focus. A balanced lifestyle is quite possibly out of the picture, and even worse, they have lost that connection with themselves to the chaotic and hectic lifestyle they lead. It becomes harder to find happiness and easier for emotions to get the best of us is that situation, which is why it becomes increasingly more difficult to find a sense of calm with everything that is going on.

The amount of stress that builds up inside of us is exactly why meditation is needed to help regain that sense of control in your life. Control how you react to what is going on around you, to focus and be clear again, be mindful, be aware and more importantly, feel calm in a situation that could easily cause a lot of grief and stress to you.

Meditation to relieve stress

Feeling calmness and serenity begins with reconnecting with your inner self and being one with your mind and your body again - taking care of yourself from the inside, which is an area that may have been neglected. Other benefits that you will gain from making meditation a regular part of your routine include the following:

Increase your mindfulness and self-awareness by connecting your mind and body.

You are provided with the techniques that you need to help regulate your emotions whenever you feel like they are getting out of control. Meditation will help you sharpen your focus, which will then enhance your mental clarity and levels of concentration.

It provides you with the techniques that you need to collect your thoughts in moments of stress, and over time, you will begin to develop the ability to block out anything that is going to prove to be a stress factor, so you will feel calmer.

Meditation for calmness will eventually lead to happiness because your mind is not constantly worked up and focused on the stress that you are experiencing. By regulating your mood to minimize your stress levels, you will be helping your body increase its serotonin production, which will then help you to feel better.

Feeling calm requires being mindful, which is what guided meditation will teach you and when you are more mindful, you will be able to better focus on the things you have to be grateful for, instead of the things that stress you out.

Not only will meditation be the tool that helps you feel calm, but the overall benefits that you feel from the entire meditational practice will help you develop a better sense of wellbeing overall. This makes it easier for you to feel much happier in the long run. Your new sense of wellbeing will then help you overcome the obstacles in your life - no matter what they may be - because you won't be feeling emotionally unseated any longer.

Here are some useful meditations that may work for you to relieve stress. Not all of these meditations may be something that you are comfortable with. Try them all but only continue with what is comfortable and fits your needs.

Chocolate Meditation

Chocolate! I'm feeling much better already! This meditation can be completed in a few minutes. Chocolate meditation is all about engaging your senses all at once and then subsequently losing yourself in them. It's like how you eat a delicious dessert. This meditation is all about savoring your present senses and emotions.

Loving Kindness Meditation

This type of meditation has amazing benefits for stress management and helps you in your journey to achieve overall life satisfaction. This meditation focuses on the feel-good scenario with your close friends, family members, and people you love and trust. It is about joining the people you trust and meditating together, connecting with one mind.

Music Meditation

Music can affect both our physiology as well as our emotions. For this meditation, you need to be in a room with only peaceful, serene music. Either lie flat on the floor with your palms facing outwards or sit comfortably on the floor with your legs crossed and your palms resting on your thighs or the floor. Use the music as your focal point and immerse yourself in the auditory experience.

Bath Meditation

This meditation uses water, bath salts, and even aromatherapy. It is a form of self-care that is encouraged at least once a week. Draw yourself a nice, hot bath and sprinkle two cups of epsom salt inside. Light up your favorite aromatherapy candles and immerse yourself in the hot tub. Close your eyes and either practice mindful meditation or focus on your breathing. Let go of all the thoughts of your stressful day and let your mind go free - you want it to be in a state of blankness without having any thoughts. You need only 15 minutes for this meditation.

Yoga Meditations

Get into a comfortable and easy sitting pose, legs crossed on the floor. Next, curl your fingertips into your palm and extend your thumbs. Next, lift your arms to a 60-degree angle aiming each over your head. Here hold your breath of fire with your eyes closed for a minimum of 1 minute to a maximum of 3 minutes. End this pose by inhaling and bringing your thumbs to touch over your head. Exhale and open your fingers.

Reach for your toes - Starting from an easy pose, spread your legs wide, comfortably - Your feet should be flexed. Next, lift your arms over your head, stretching your spine from the base, then exhale down to the left and touch your toes if possible. From here, inhale back to the center an Exhale down to the right. Continue doing this for a minimum of 1 minute to a maximum of 3 minutes.

Hold your toes- Sit with your legs wide open and reach out to hold the toes on both of your feet. If this is uncomfortable, you can modify by holding your shins. Next, exhale and bring your hands to the floor, then from here allow your torso and head to follow. Breath deeply and feel your stretch. Do this for one to three minutes.

Grasp your shins- Come into a cross-legged position and grasp your shins. Inhale deeply and flex your spine forward followed by an exhale to flex the spine backward. Maintain your head level and your arms slightly straight. Keep your form relaxed for about one to three minutes.

Rock Pose - From an easy pose shift to a rock pose and sit on your heels. Let your hands lay flat on your thighs and continue to flex your spine by rolling forward during the inhale and rolling backward during the exhale. Keep your eyes closed and gently rolled towards the third eye. Continue for 1-3 minutes.

Grasp your shoulders- Sit on your heels and align your torso and head forward. Lift your arms up gently and grasp your shoulders. Your fingers should be in front with your thumbs behind. Next, inhale and twist to the left and when exhaling twist to the right. Make sure to keep your arms lifted with your upper arm parallel to the floor.

Shoulder lifts - Sit in an easy pose and allow your hands to rest on your knees gently. Start by inhaling and lifting your left shoulder, exhaling and lifting the right shoulder while lowering the left. Continue this for one minute by alternating the shoulder lifts and then reverse your breath as well as the movement, this time inhaling by lifting the right shoulder and exhaling by lifting the left shoulder.

Lift both shoulders - In this pose, move by lifting your shoulders together inhaling and exhaling for 1 minute.

Turn your head- Still sitting in your easy pose, place your hands on your knees and turn your head to the left inhaling and then turning it to the right exhaling. Continue this for one minute making sure to keep your head level as you turn from side to side. Next, reverse your breath and your gaze so when you inhale you turn your head to the right and when you exhale you turn your head to the left. Continue for 1 more minute then inhale deeply, suspend the breath and focus at the third eye. Slowly exhale and relax.

Laya Yoga Meditation- This last sequence closes with a meditation known as "Laya Yoga Meditation." Stay in a seated easy pose with your wrists dressing on your knees and your hands doing a Gyan Mudra (thumb tip and index finger tip touching).

Savasana -Finally relax into a savasana and meditate on balance, wholeness and the 10 bodies.

Meditation to Remove Anxiety

When there is chaos, we need to give our immediate attention to it - to run away from the chaos, remove yourself from it, deal with it, or try to rectify it. Either way, chaos needs to be paid attention to, unlike peace and serenity that doesn't demand our attention. When we have chaos in our life, it sucks the energy out of us and keeps us on high stress. However, with meditation, you can use the stillness and quietness in your mind to subdue chaos and allow your thoughts to be more focused and positive. Through meditation, you can deal with chaos in a more constructive way, and it also allows the answers to deal with chaos come easily to you.

The goal for meditation to relieve anxiety is to let go of our emotions and reactions to observe from a detached perspective. With meditation, you teach yourself to observe without assigning emotion to any given situation. All you need to do is watch with a blank state of mind.

Meditation also exercises your mind to have a better sense of awareness of the present, while still staying in control of any negativity that may come and prevent it from increasing. Meditation heightens the brain's cognitive function through mood training and mental training, which can alleviate anxiety and decrease stress levels. It also teaches us to respond reflectively and not reflexively. In doing so, not only do we prevent anxiety, we also prevent depression and other mood disorders.

Waking Up Peacefully

Nobody likes the sound of their alarm going off, especially if the alarm is a harsh, long, and loud ringing sound that jolts you out of your slumber. Changing your waking up pattern by changing your alarm clock sound. If you are like everyone else who uses their mobile phones, use an app that tracks sleeping patterns such as the sleep analysis feature on the iPhone. Choose a wake-up sound that is soothing rather than loud and abrasive. Sounds of nature, birds chirping or a mantra as a wake up sound helps to gradually wake you up rather than giving you an abrupt wake up. Waking up peacefully helps lessen any chaos that comes into your mind the minute your eyes open.

Breathing Practice

One of the first few things you can do in your meditation is learn to breathe correctly when you meditate. It isn't about just breathing in and out. It is about controlling your breathing so that it is in line with your mindfulness.

As you wake up peacefully, stretch your body, elongate and lengthen it so that energy passes through you from the top of your head to the tips of your fingers. While doing so, breathe in deeply through your nose and exhale through your mouth. Fill your lungs with air. This helps balance the body's sympathetic and parasympathetic responses towards anxiety as well as stress.

Deep breathing also enables the body's relaxation response, reducing cortisol - the stress hormone. Mindfully breathing for at least 5 minutes in the morning can dramatically improve any symptoms that are anxiety related and also lessen stress as well as panic attacks.

Bringing in Consciousness to the Body

A core element of meditation is practicing awareness at the present moment. If you are worried about what could happen, what will happen, or what has happened, anxiety will start to creep on you because you are not aware that you cannot control the past or the future.

When you feel thoughts like this coming to your mind, remove yourself from the situation you are in and head to a quiet place. Either sit or stand and just ground yourself in the present time. Focus on your breathing and pay attention to the sensations you are experiencing. Zero your focus into something specific that makes you calm inside so that you can quiet down your racing thoughts. Take this time to be conscious of your surroundings and feelings, then slowly open your eyes and bring awareness to your body. Do this only when you feel your heart beating at a normal pace. If not, continue this exercise until you feel calm and centered.

Check In With Your Body

Sometimes, the symptoms for anxiety happen suddenly without warning. Whenever you feel your hands start sweating, your heart racing, and your muscles tightening, step away from what you are doing and take a 5-second break to reconnect with your body. Conduct a Body scan to systematically check-in with your body parts. You can do this either by sitting on a chair or lying down on a mat. Allow yourself to relax and during this process, observe the contact between your body and the mat or chair.

Check where you feel the pressure. Bring awareness and contact to the different points in your body but do not associate it with any pain, emotion, or discomfort. Begin with your head and scan your body from the top to the bottom. Do not label any feelings or any emotions but only observe. When you take note of a tense spot, think of it for a bit and then simply move on. Continue breathing and allow your breathing to guide you as you scan your body.

Release any muscle tension while you give yourself time to restart.

Yoga Meditation

Once again yoga can be your best ally even to relieve excesses of anxiety. This meditation is everything you need- it is your teacher and your best friend. It will help you readjust and realign your balance into your mind and by extension, your life.

For this meditation, you are sorting through everything from breaking habits to achieving your emotional balance. If you have been emotionally upset and do not have any idea why, this mediation can help you feel relaxed and whole again. This meditation also helps you focus and center your person. It is a catalyst that causes change, simply because it is an extremely powerful spiritual cleanser.

If you have been going through a lot, you may also be releasing alot. Be willing to let it all go and also be present to what you are experiencing through the meditation. The process will also enable you to clear out all your toxicity. This meditation is great for those who want to change and bring in a new dimension into your life. All you have to do is trust in the meditation process as well as the energy that comes.

Directions:

Start this meditation by sitting with a straight spine, stacked. Once you feel relaxed and focused, start chanting SA TA NA MA. While you are chanting, press your thumb with four fingers alternately. Use enough pressure and keep pressing to keep yourself awake but stay aware of the pressure you are putting. Keep repeating this in a stable rhythm and keep the hand motion going consistently throughout the whole meditation.

Chant SA and press the thumb and the first finger together with pressure. The first finger draws in knowledge, and expands our possibilities, ridding us from limitations.

TA press the thumb and the middle finger together. The middle finger gives us patience, purity, and wisdom.

NA press the thumb and the ring finger together. The ring finger is all about vitality and aliveness.

MA press the thumb and the small finger together. The little finger brings in better communication.

Each time a mudra is closed by joining the thumb with a finger your ego seals off the effect in your consciousness.

Feel and visualize each sound that comes into your crown chakra, traveling down to the middle of your head and out to the beyond through the third eye. This is extremely important and must be conducted with each sound. It is an integral part of the process of cleansing. Without this meditation sequence, you will end up having a headache.

Also, during this meditation, you may experience images of the past that come into your mind like a movie reel. Allow these images to dance in front of your eyes but with each mantra that you do, release them. This sequence is clearing the subconscious mind. If any emotions come up to you now, infuse them into your mantra and chanting. All these things that are happening- the emotions, the images - all of this is very normal to experience. Never try to control these experiences because it will only cause negative implications. Just trust in the process and go through it willingly.

Timing - 31 Minute Version

- Chant out loud for the first 5 minutes.

- Chant in an audible whisper for the second 5 minutes.

- Chant silently for the next 10 minutes. Keep your hands, L in the head and tongue moving.

- Chant in a whisper for the next 5 minutes.

- Chant out loud for the last 5 minutes.

The last minute, listen inside and hear the mantra and experience the L in the head. Do not do the finger movements. This mantra should be done for exactly 31 minutes for optimum results. You can also do this mantra for a maximum of 62 minutes by doubling the chanting times.

Chapter 9: Setting Goals and Your Mood Board

***

Setting your fitness goals when you begin a routine is key to ensuring that you sustain this lifestyle for the long run. Setting goals is a tricky process, if they are too easy you may end up losing interest, and it won't be challenging for you. Too hard and you can become easily demotivated when you don't achieve them.

So to keep you focused on your goals here are some tips for getting those goals in place:

1. **Set one goal at a time** – Never bite off more than you can chew. The one biggest mistake we do is trying to accomplish so much in a small amount of time. This is especially true when you are starting something new. Pick goals that you see yourself accomplishing and tackle them one at a time.

2. **Using the SMART approach** – Smart, Measurable, Attainable, Realistic and Time-Based. When setting goals, you need to utilize this methodology. As the meaning of the acronym suggests, by using this methodology, you will create goals that are logical, measurable and have a period that will ensure your progress can be tracked and monitored. One example of using "SMART" for setting goals is by starting off running at an easy pace for 10 minutes and slowly and gradually increasing your time by 1 extra minute every alternate day for the course of 30 days.

3. **Keeping the bar low** – Just like the "SMART" approach, your goal needs to be attainable. It should be easy but not too easy. It should be challenging so that you will start to see progress in your overall health and fitness. Be confident when you set the goal and believe that you can achieve it. Having goals that are attainable at the early stage when you are starting will allow you to be more motivated to stick to your fitness journey. Having this early success is vital to building motivation and confidence for you in the long run.

4. **Don't compare** – It is easy to become discouraged when building your fitness journey by comparing yourself with other individuals on social media, especially when you are first starting out. Always remember, everyone starts somewhere, so don't get discouraged by someone else's progress but focus on your journey.

5. **Always remember what is driving you** – Always keep in mind why got you started on this fitness journey. With the same determination that you have at work, try to channel that similar drive to motivate you to achieve the goals you have set yourself.

6. **Results Take Time** – Just as in business, success takes time and the same relates to your fitness goals. It takes weeks and even months to see the desired changes that you wanted for yourself at both a physical and mental level. Having a long-term mindset will allow you to see your goal as a change to your lifestyle instead of an intermittent fix.

When setting your goals, you can also employ the use of mood boards to arrange your journey. A mood board is an arrangement of pictures, materials, and texts that are collected as a basis of creative information, to prepare for a project. However, mood boards do not need to be just pictures, they can also include video and sound as well. Here are some tips on creating a mood board using an app known as *Milanote.*

1. **Have a clear objective** – You can choose your board to be either literal or practical or it can be made to explore tones or moods – You can combine the two to achieve your final outlay.

2. **Choose your direction** – Keep an open mind when creating your mood board. It's all about exploring your theme and seeing what best fits you.

3. **Add in written inspirations** – Before adding in your pictures, add in any text that is relevant towards the objective of your goals. Taglines, words of wisdom and any inspirational text can be included at this point.

4. **Images** – No you can add in any photos and visual that is in line with your objective. Any images that may spark motivation for your fitness journey can be added in at this stage. Try to use as many pictures as you can and don't worry about arranging them in a pattern that will come later.

5. **Source the web for designs** – Go online to look for any free visual inspiration that you can incorporate into your mood board. Search for images that connect with your objective and theme. Some sites that provide these images are Dribble, Behance and Designinspiration. Use proper keywords when looking for these designs.

6. **Use of colors and fonts** – Using tools like Kuler can be great at adding mood and personality to your mood board. Choosing the right color palettes will be an excellent way to express the feeling you are trying to convey in your mood board. It is also essential to ensure the colors you select complement each other and are visually appealing.

7. **Use photos** – Photos are a great way to showcase your thoughts and complement the overall theme of your mood board. Websites like Pexels, iStockPhoto and the Creative Commons offer free photos that you can incorporate into

your design.

8. **Composition and balance** – Once you have all your media, you can start arranging them into your final idea. Play around a bit and see what fits. Make changes where required to fit your desired objective. Although a mood board is for communicating your visual thoughts, it's going to need some explanation before it makes sense to someone who sees it. You can add short notes to explain certain things on your board if you need to. Embedding these notes in a board keeps everything in context.

Chapter 10: Exercise Routines That Are Perfect For Travelling

***

Traveling for work does not need to be a stressful endeavor, and it should not get in the way of your daily exercise routine. This is especially important if you have to travel for extended periods of time across states or even overseas. If you don't plan for these long trips, bad habits will start to creep and will affect the progress you have made all this while. Plus restarting a routine after a long break will be a bit more daunting over time. Keeping yourself active during these long trips can help you stay focused and reap the benefits that we previously discussed from exercises.

Here are some tips that we can share with you that you can utilize during your business travels to maintain your fitness.

Pack the Essentials

Research the area that you will be visiting for recreation parks or nearby gyms. Better yet, check if the hotel you'll be staying in comes with a gym that you can use during your stay. Many hotels have gyms or pools, or offer day passes to local fitness centers.

Then pack your exercise essentials based on the following equipment's:

- Workout shoes.

- Workout clothes.

- Swimwear (depending on the choice of your activity).

- Jump rope or resistance bands.

- Yoga Mat.

Also, make sure you pack your headphones so that you can use them with your handphone while you workout. Pack as many essentials as you deemed fit based on the duration of your stay and accessibility to local fitness areas.

Try To Keep Active

When you travel, you are bound to be sitting for long periods of time, which can be detrimental to your health and posture. But you can still fit in some simple physical activity during your commute to negate this effect. When you're at the airport waiting for your plane, try to take a walk around the terminal while waiting for time to board. If you're traveling by train, try walking in between the coaches instead of just sitting around. If you're driving, stop at periodic intervals to get a break and do some light stretching. And when you arrive at your destination and have time before your meeting, try to take a walk to have a quick workout. If that isn't possible, then make sure to plan your next exercise when the time permits it.

Here are some additional tips to being active during this traveling time:

Swimming – A great cardio workout and many hotels have a pool in which you can get a few laps in.

Jump Rope – Another simple exercise that can be done at the convenience of your hotel room and you just need a skipping rope

Jumping Jacks – Another excellent cardio activity to get the heartbeat pumping and body sweating.

If the above tips are a bit too easy for your liking, here are some exercise routines that are equipment- free, require minimal space, and only need your bodyweight:

#1. Arm Challenge that also targets your core, shoulders and back muscles:

- 10 Plank Ups.

- 10 Lateral Plank Walks.

- 10 Burpees With Push Ups.

- 10 Planks With Shoulder Taps.

- 10 Diamond Push Ups.

- 10 Mountain Climbers.

Repeat for 3 rounds.

#2. For stronger glutes, try this routine:

- Side-Step Squats.

- Single Leg Glute Bridges.

- Curtsy Lunges With Side Lick.

Do 12-15 reps for each exercise (both sides). Rest 90 seconds in between exercises.

#3. 10 Minute Cardio Morning Workout

- Burpee With Push.

- Squat Jump.

- Plank With Shoulder Tap.

- Jumping Lunge.

- Repeat for 2 rounds.

- Pick Your Intensity.

- Beginner – 30 secs on, 30 secs off.

- Intermediate – 40 secs on, 20 secs off.

- Expert – 50 seconds on, 10 secs off.

#4. 10 Minute Total Body Workout

- Bodyweight Squats.

- Push-Ups.

- Plank With T-Rotation.

- Alternating Standing Oblique Crunches.

Do each move for 2 minutes and take a 30 second rest after each exercise.

#5. 10 Minute Leg Day Workout

- Plie Squat With One Foot Raised – 30 seconds each side.

- Alternating Side Lunges – 30 seconds each side.

- Skater Hops – 15 seconds.

- Curtsy Kicks – 30 seconds each side.

- Goblet Squat – 30 seconds.

- Jumping Jacks – 30 seconds.

- Pilates Scissors – 30 seconds.

- Clamshells – 30.

Do each move for 2 minutes and take a 30 second rest after each exercise.

#6. Core Workout

- Step It Up.

- Leg Lift.

- Tap It Out.

- Downward Dog Reach.

Do 2 sets of 10 reps each.

#7. 20 Minute Cardio Circuit

- Jumping Lunges.

- Wall Sit With Hands Up.

- Jumping Squats.

- Plank.

Do 1 minute of each exercise with one minute rest till the 20 minutes are up

#8. Travel Friendly Cardio Workout

- 30 second Air Punches, 5 Burpees.

- 30 second Air Punches, 4 Burpees.

- 30 second Air Punches, 3 Burpees.

- 30 second Air Punches, 2 Burpees.

- 30 second Air Punches, 1 Burpees.

- 30 second Air Punches, 2 Burpees.

- 30 second Air Punches, 3 Burpees.

- 30 second Air Punches, 4 Burpees.

- 30 second Air Punches, 5 Burpees.

☆ If you have gotten this far and have achieved more than you thought possible, please consider leaving a short review for the book on Amazon. Thank you!

Chapter 11: Creating a Healthy Morning and Night Routine

***

Warren Buffet wakes up at 6.45am and begins his day with reading.

Former First Lady, **Michelle Obama** starts her morning routine with exercise.

Anna Wintour, Vogue Editor-in-Chief begins her day at 5.45am with a vigorous tennis match.

John Paul Dejoria, entrepreneur and self-made billionaire begins with a 5 minute morning meditation and reflecting all the things he is grateful for.

Naveen Jain, CEO of InfoSpace begins his day at4.30am and focuses on catching up with the news, reading emails as well as meditation.

So what is your take away, as an entrepreneur, from all of these routines?

All of the people mentioned above have one thing in common-they make sure that they prioritize their physical and mental health, from meditation, taking time to appreciate achievements, focusing on goals, working out- these are all ways that you can transform your mental and physical capacity to do more, and be more.

Another thing they share in common- they all stick to their routine no matter where they are. They know what needs to be done and how sticking to their routines is both a reflection of their self-discipline as well as their self-respect.

This positive beginning sets the tone for the rest of the day.

If you have not thought about your morning routine, now is the time to. Your sleeping and waking up patterns will define how the rest of your day will be and how it influences your business as well.

Here is how you can start. This chapter gives you an example of how you can craft your sleeping and morning routines but tweak them to fit your own needs.

Morning Routine

1. Start by waking up at least one hour earlier than your usual time.

2. Make your bed. Military training always places importance on soldiers making their bed perfectly. The reason is simply that you've accomplished one task in the morning!

3. Drink a glass of lemon water. Lemon water in the morning is known to boost energy and brain power.

4. Do some light stretching to get your blood pumping and awaken your senses.

5. Listen to your favorite songs during shower. Songs give you a better mood to kick off the day!

6. Look at your vision board!

Night Routine

Bedtime is more of a time to reflect. It is a time for you to calm your senses and switch off from the world.

1. Start by switching off. Research shows that you should stop looking at your digital devices 15 minutes before you go to sleep.

2. Do some light stretching to relax and soothe yourself.

3. Say a prayer, do some reflection or just meditate in savasana.

4. Kiss your partner/spouse and children goodnight.

5. Breathe deeply, through a long inhale and a slow exhale while keeping your eyes closed. This will enable you to fall into a deep sleep, faster.

Reflection exercises you can do:

Reflect not on what is going to happen but instead, look at the things that have already taken place. Mentally go through the things that happened in your day and ask yourself:

- Did you behave according to your principles?

- Have you treated the people with whom you interacted with in a friendly and considerate manner?

- What vices did you fight?

- Did you make yourself a better person by cultivating your virtues?

You can also write down your reflections and you can also plan the next day. Write down your notes and what you want to reflect on in the morning. What you do today will link up with tomorrow morning's reflection.

In your journal, write down what you want to improve on the next day. It doesn't have to be a big thing. Write it down no matter how small the improvement may be. If you keep this up for 21 days, you'd be surprised how much you can and would be able to change.

Along with your notes, also remind yourself that this day has ended and there is no way you can change anything about it unless you time traveled. What has happened, has happened. The sun will rise tomorrow.

Waking Up Early

Many successful individuals and entrepreneurs credit their accomplishments to getting up early. They state that, early-risers have more productive mornings and are able to accomplish more activities than those that get up later in the day. The one reason many of them advocate getting up early to increase productivity is that there aren't any distractions that can derail you from getting any tasks completed. If you're planning on getting up between 4:00 am and 5:00 am, many others in your time zone are still asleep. Hence, you won't get unnecessary calls or emails, and your kids or spouse won't be disturbing you. You can use the calmness of the morning to get your day going smoothly.

Tips on waking up early

However, for many of us, the thought of getting out of bed in the wee hours of the morning can seem formidable. However, here are five tips to help you get yourself out of bed at 5:00 am and kick start your day:

1. Keep your alarm clock as far away as possible - Don't keep your alarm clock within arm's reach of you. If you do this, you can quickly turn it off and go back to sleep. It is advised that you position your alarm clock (or your mobile phone, if you're using the alarm app) far away from your bed so that you will physically have to get up and out of bed to turn it off. Some have even placed their alarm clocks in other rooms so that once you're up, you are not going back to bed again. One example is to keep your alarm clock or mobile phone in the bathroom. That way, once you turn it off, you can easily and quickly take a shower and freshen up to get started on your day. You can also opt for a more drastic measure by setting up multiple alarm clocks to wake you up.

2. Stop using the snooze button - The snooze button has not helped anyone in getting up when they need to. We advise getting an alarm clock without the snooze button function. Or if you already have an alarm clock with a snooze button, try to make it redundant. This should stop you from relying on it and get you up when you need to.

3. Change your alarm buzzer frequently - When you end up using the same buzzer or alarm tone every day, you start to build immunity or tolerance towards the sound. As such, it becomes harder and harder to get up each day. Try to reset the tone of the alarm every other week so that you do not become accustomed to one single sound. If you change your tone frequently, you'll have a higher chance of getting up early.

4. Making a puzzle - If locating your phone at a different location or changing your alarm tone doesn't help in getting up early, try making it harder for you to turn it off. Here are a few tips, try placing your alarm clock in a hard to reach place or inside a cupboard or drawer that you can lock. Better yet, get a simple safe that needs a combination to unlock it. If you have to force yourself or struggle to turn your alarm off, you'll be completely awake once you get this done.

5. Have a goal or reason - Keep yourself motivated to get up early by having a purpose. It'll be tough to get up early if there isn't any reason in mind to do so. But if you have a reason or goal to do so, you'll be even more motivated to jump out of bed and get things done. So set yourself a task to do first thing in the morning. It can be from getting some exercise in or watering your plants or taking the dog for a walk. But more importantly, have a goal in mind to keep you motivated, and the rest will fall in place quickly.

6. Sleep on time - Getting ample rest for about seven to eight hours, as well as cutting out alcohol and caffeine before bedtime can help you in getting enough rest and being able to get up early.

Exercising- Conquering your demons at the start of the day

We all know that having a healthy lifestyle can bring a lot of benefits to the well-being of your body in the long term. But research has also shown that implementing exercise into your daily routine can boost your productivity levels and creativity, as well as your focus throughout the entire day.

A study was conducted on about 150 employees randomly selected from three different companies, and over a few weeks, they were observed and evaluated on days without exercise and with exercise.

It showed that on days these individuals exercised, they had scored 20% higher for concentration at work, 22% higher for completing tasks before deadlines and 25% higher completing a job without taking breaks. Amazingly, all these individuals stated that they had a higher motivation to work on days that they included exercise in their daily activities. Many kinds of research have shown that having a daily workout routine does significantly increase an employee's work performance, thus leading to high levels of productivity.

Now, where do we start or more precisely what type of exercise should we focus on, for increasing productivity?

You might be thinking that a strenuous workout just before the workday would be the best to pump you up. But studies have shown that it is untrue. On the contrary, low-impact and low-intensity workouts seem to be the best way to ignite your productivity levels. If you opt for workouts with high intensity, you may experience higher fatigue levels than a low-intensity exercise.

In one study, it was shown that after a high-intensity workout that comprised of weights and cardio, test subjects started to show dips in problem-solving, focus, and memory. These effects continued for another 20- 30 minutes. Another group that was put in a much lower intensity exercise was shown to have not been affected.

Any exercise such as yoga, cycling, or jogging can be an excellent start. If you're still not sure, try walking 10,000 steps each day (not at one go). Now comes the next question, when do you exercise? In the morning before going to work or in the evening? As the day progresses, your strength levels increase, but we are more concerned about increasing your productivity and not your strength. And productivity levels are tied to your mood and energy throughout the day.

It'll be best to plan your workout first thing in the morning as opposed to the evenings. Keep your workout sessions around 30 minutes each time but do not do anything for less than 10 minutes.

Sticking to a habit can be a tricky thing, especially when you have to do it first thing in the morning. But it's better to get a workout done for even 10 minutes a day than to never do anything at all. Once you have chosen your go to work out, you can follow these steps to help build a routine and start improving your productivity:

- Take small steps – Do not overexert yourself at the start of your exercise routine. Take small progressive steps and improve on them day by day. For example, if you plan of walking non-stop for 30 minutes, try to walk for 1 minute and take a rest for 1 minute and repeat that 15 times. Then slowly build your endurance gradually till you've managed to reach your goal.

- Remember to have fun – Choose an exercise or workout routine that you like. You want to avoid following a pattern that is going to bore you in the long run.

- Have few obstacles – At the start, don't push yourself to look into nutrition or how many calories you'll be burning off. Focus on the small steps and eliminate possible barriers that will prevent you from making progress.

- Plan ahead – Keep a reminder of days that you need to

exercise on your mobile phone or calendar and stick to it. Once you keep this routine going, it'll become a daily part of your life.

SECTION 3: CULTIVATING GOOD MENTAL HABITS

Cultivating mental habits is written towards the end of the book because changing the way we think is probably not as easy as we believe. However, once we start tweaking the easier things such as eating right and exercising every morning, we benefit the mind. What we once thought was hard to do, is now simple, and you're left with a feeling of astonishment that you haven't tried this before. Conquering your mind, your thoughts, and the way you think is the final step in becoming a holistically successful entrepreneur.

Chapter 12: Positive Thinking is important to cultivate better social skills and influence people

***

If you listed ten things today – seven of them were things that made you happy, and three made you unhappy, sad, frustrated or moody – then most likely you were grateful, and you were positive. The thing is, many of us would prefer to be happy and positive rather than be unhappy and negative. And it is that simple to be positive and happy. Also, positive thinking is above and beyond just being happy or displaying a cheerful and upbeat attitude. It also creates and establishes value in your life and relationships, and helps you build skills that benefit you for the long run. Barbara Fredrickson, a positive psychology researcher from the University of North Carolina, published a landmark paper on the impact of positive thinking on work, health, and general wellbeing. Here's a brief explanation of Barbara's research:

What Can Negative Thinking do to your Brain?

Our brain is programmed to respond to negative emotions by shutting off the world around us and limiting the options we see around us. For example, if you get into a fight with your sister, your emotions and anger might consume you to the point where you react adversely – you can't think about anything else. Or for instance, your coffee this morning spilled on your shirt, and this creates a domino effect of everything going wrong in your day, and you get so stressed out that you find it hard to start or do anything because you've lost your focus. Or if you are supposed to complete a project, but you didn't, you begin to feel bad about it, and all you think of is how irresponsible you are, that you are lazy, and you lack motivation. The point is, our brain shuts off from the outside world and relies on the negative emotions of fear, stress, and anger. Negative thoughts and feelings prevent us from seeing other options, solutions, or choices that are around us.

What Can Positive Thinking do to your Brain?

Barbara Fredrickson also explains how positive thinking manifests in our brain. She explains with an experiment where research subjects are divided into five groups, and each group is shown a different video clip. The first group was shown clips that created feelings of joy whereas the second group was shown clips that created contentment, the third was the control group that had images of no significant emotions and were neutral whereas group four had clips that created fear and group five had clips that created the feelings of anger.

Participants were then asked to imagine themselves in situations that these same emotions would come about and write down their reactions to it. Participants that viewed images of fear and anger had the least responses or reactions whereas participants who saw joy and contentment had more results. The bottom line is, if you experience positive emotions you will see more possibilities in life. Positive emotions broaden our possibilities and thinking, thus opening up more options for us in facing issues, crisis, problems, and solutions and so on.

In the next few chapters, we will discuss how we can work our mind to be more positive and look at things in a more positive perspective to enhance and give more value to our life, relationships, and goals. It is not as hard as it seems because all it takes is a little practice.

A positive mind is a state of mind that is worth developing because everyone, entrepreneur or not, can benefit from it and who knows where it will take you.

A Positive attitude is noticeable in the following ways:

- Positive thinking.

- Constructive thinking.

- Creative thinking.

- Optimism.

- Drive and energy to do things, accomplish goals.

- An attitude of happiness.

A positive mindset can help you in many ways:

- Expecting success as failure is not an option.

- The feeling of inspiration in everything you do.

- Gives you the strength to keep going and not give up.

- Helps you overcome obstacles you face.

- Gives you the ability to look at failures, mistakes, and problems as a blessing in disguise.

- Keeps you believing in yourself, your abilities, and your talent.

- Radiate self-esteem and confidence.

- You look for solutions instead of dwelling on problems, you seek opportunities when it comes.

- Positive thinking is a game changer- you can change your whole life if you always look on the bright side instead of wallowing in self-pity and allowing yourself to think negatively.

- Positive thinking is infectious! It not only affects you but each individual around you- people want to be with you, make friends with you and hang out with you because you've got the drive, energy and positivity, making it so easy to be your friend. You will end up changing the lives of those around you, uplifting them and encouraging them to become the best version of themselves. Positivity is a strong emotion so if you are positive; you radiate positivity.

Even more benefits of a Positive Attitude for the Entrepreneurial Spirit:

- You achieve more of your goals easily

- You achieve success much rapidly.

- You bring in more happiness in your life and those around you.

- You have more energy to deal with everything life throws at you.

- You have more faith in your abilities and have higher hopes for a brighter future.

- You can inspire and motivate everyone around you.

- You feel you encounter fewer obstacles and difficulties compared to other people.

- You are much more respected and loved by all those around you.

- Life smiles at you.

The bottom line is, if you exhibit a negative attitude then you will only bring in more failure and more difficulties but if you radiate positivity, you are bound to be attracting good energy and success. The time is NOW to change the way you think and the way you react.

Negative thoughts, behaviors and reactions do nobody any good. If you have tried to become positive in the past but you have failed, that means you have not tried enough.

Exercises for Every Morning

One of the best things to start a more positive lifestyle is to create a set of routines.

Here are a collection of things you can do to start your day right:

- Have 7 to 8 hours of sleep.

- When the alarm rings, wake up, stretch but never hit the Snooze button (it takes practice).

- Drink a glass of water with a slice of lemon.

- Listen to some music while you shower (helps alleviate your mood)..

- Eat breakfast! (smoothies, oatmeal or a breakfast muffin is easy and fast to make ahead)

- Smile to your mirror!

- Head out the door and tell yourself- I'm ready to take on the world!

Positive thinking is applied in many different fields from business to sales, marketing to advertising, health, sports, education, motivation, inspiration, national allegiance, psychology as well as self-image.

Many of the twenty-first-century authors apply positive thinking in various areas. Some of these famous ones are:

- **_Anthony Robbins_**' seminar and speeches using the knowledge of psychology and positive thinking. Robbins' is a motivational speaker and advisor to many world leaders and have helped ordinary people to achieve success or lead a more positive and fulfilling life.

- **_Steven Covey_** is the author of 'The 7 Habits of Highly Effective People', and his points are regularly quotes in businesses and personal development. These seven habits can be used above and beyond the business realm, applying it to almost anything in life.

- **_Louise Hay_** is the author of 'You can Heal Your Life' and several other motivational and self-improvement books. She promotes the use of self-healing to use the power of our thoughts to enhance our lives.

- **_Wayne W. Dyer_** employs the teaching of Tao Te Ching of 'Change your thoughts, change your life' which directly influences use to lead and live a more balanced and fulfilling lifestyle. Dryer is the author of 'The Power of Intention.

Creating Positive Social Goals towards better social skills

Social goals are essential because it helps you attain other goals that you have in your life.

- Make a conscious effort to smile at the people you meet..

- Say good morning to your colleagues.

- Laugh as much as you can, and don't take yourself too seriously. Laughter is bonding.

- Invest in personal hygiene and new clothes. Showering and grooming help you stay alert and focused and ready for challenges that the day has for you.

- Do not complain or gossip and let go of gripe. Remove yourself from negative situations.

- Stretch as much as you can- even at work. Rolling your shoulders, stretching your leg and little exercises help you open up and breathe better.

Empathy in real life (not as shown to us in the movies)

Empathy is the ability to recognize how people would feel towards a specific scenario, thing, or person. Having this ability is crucial to success both in your career and life. The more you can decipher the feelings of people, the better you can manage the thoughts and approaches you send them.

Empathetic people are excellent at:

- Recognizing, anticipating and meeting a person's needs.

- Developing the needs of other people and bolstering their individual abilities.

- Taking advantage of diversity by cultivating opportunities among different people.

- Developing political awareness by understanding the current emotional state of people and fostering powerful relationships.

- Focusing on identifying feelings and wants of other people.

Developing good interpersonal skills is imperative as well if you want a successful life and career. In our world today, when plenty of things are digitized, social skills seem to be an afterthought. People skills are more relevant and sought-after then before, especially since now you also need a high EQ to understand, negotiate and empathize with others – primarily if you deal and interact with different people daily.

Among the most useful skills are:

- Influence to effectively wield persuasive tactics.

- Communication to send out clear and concise messages.

- Leadership to inspire and guide people and groups.

- Change catalyst in kick-starting and managing change.

- Managing conflicting situations which includes the ability to negotiate, understand, and resolve disagreements.

- To bond and nurture meaningful relationships.

- Teamwork, cooperation, and collaboration in meeting shared goals.

- Creating a synergetic group to work towards collective goals.

Chapter 13: Thinking based on different interlocutors

Firstly, let's explore what interlocutors are. In the world of linguistics and discourse analysis, interlocutors are people that are involved in a dialogue or conversation. When two or more people are engaged in a conversation with one another, they are each other's interlocutors. In more layman terms, an interlocutor can also be referred to as a conversation partner, addressee, or hearer.

In the age of instant communication, it makes it much easier to speak to people, no matter who they are. You can simultaneously 'speak' to several people at different times. For example, you can be typing an email, and speaking to a friend on Skype, sending a message on Whatsapp, and also talking to your colleague next to you. How effective are these communications you are having, and are you able to address the issues, answer the questions, and give the proper solutions to all these interlocutors?

It is crucial to keep in mind that technology should be used to create effective dialogues. If you are open to communication coming from the minds of other people, then you are also able to create meaning and purpose from the virtual encounters that come into your mind, through effortless technology. Therefore, it is imperative to be personally engaged and to effectively listen to what others have to say when you navigate the frenzy of technology and non-technology interlocutors.

10 ways to think on the basis of different interlocutors

#1 'I totally understand.'

People have a strong sense of desire to connect and to hear 'Yes, I understand' really warms the heart of the people involved in the process of communication. People want to know that their message is understood and that they are not alone in their thinking. Understanding and acknowledging another person's point of view is the first step in creating the basis of successful communication. It makes both parties feel connected and reassured. The act of being present during the moment of communication means that you need to give focused attention to what the other person is saying. By paying total attention to your interlocutor, they will feel more empowered and acknowledged.

#2 'Great, tell me more about it.'

This sentence, when spoken, gives the other person a signal that you are indeed curious and interested in what the other person has to say. This phrase should be used to prioritize the dialogue, either by being silently focused or intently focusing on what they continue to say by asking the basic questions.

#3 'What do you think?'

This is an extremely powerful question because it recognizes your interlocutor's subject expertise. When you ask this question, you create a space that enables authentic suggestion from the other person. You have to be aware of the interests, ideas, and thoughts of the other person suggestion should be genuine, and you must be open to accepting these suggestions otherwise you open another line of disagreement, waste both person's time and build frustration.

#4 'I see where you are coming from.'

This is a sentence that is powerful, and it signals to the other person of your willingness to engage actively in what they are saying. When rephrasing what the other person has just formulated, you contribute to the communication flow by clarifying your understanding of the issue, and also you open up the possibility of getting more details. When you say this sentence, it benefits both interlocutors as your conversation swiftly moves into a collective meaning.

#5 'You are right.'

When this is said, people automatically feel as if they have been positively praised, especially when it is said with the utmost sincerity. Saying that you are wrong and that they are right is also a way of showing that you are a humble communicator and a person that your employees can identify with. People are more open and trusting with those that they can identify with. To tell someone that they are right will open up access to a common ground and move you towards a solution.

#6 'I trust your judgment.'

Trust combines both competence and character. Character refers to who you are as a person, whereas competence refers to what you can do effectively. Competence varies based on the context. Telling your partner or employee that you trust them is extremely meaningful, so say it when you mean it. When you tell someone you trust their judgment, this basically means that you believe in their capabilities and you acknowledge their competencies. This will lead them to feel more motivated to contribute to the project and give more creative ideas actively.

#7 'I don't know.'

Nobody has the answers to everything and acknowledging that you do not know something means you are humble but also courageous. Saying I don't know followed by a statement that follows up with a willingness to seek answers and solutions, can start up a dialogue and bond with people in a group. You can also say 'I'm not sure, but I will find out' OR 'I will think about it' tells the other person that you value their input and will consider the options as well as exercise your authority to make the right decisions. This will give you time to figure out the right solution, and your interlocutors will also see it as a sign that you are flexible and open-minded.

#8 'Thank you.'

It shows the person that you appreciate their time and investment in the conversation they had with you. It also exudes sincerity. It is the most basic code of social etiquette, and in a professional environment, this shows that you are open to engaging politely with your team. 'Please' is also another essential word in communication, and sometimes we tend to forget to say these words in the complexity of daily life. But remember to keep practicing saying 'please' and 'thank you' because it enables people to be more willing participants in the project.

#9 'Well done.'

Saying this also creates a certain warmth in the relationship between two people. It does wonders for your communication and social skills because people want to know if their idea was great and usable. If you are in a place of authority, this will enable people to work better with you as they see you as someone who appreciates good and workable ideas. They would also be more open to constructive feedback when you give praise where it is due.

#10 'I'm on it.'

This powerful display of expression is an extremely empathic one. When you say this, the person on the receiving end knows that you are committed to seeing the idea through, and it shows that you care about the project. You can also quickly win the confidence of your collaborators and partners because you have displayed a willingness to commit. When you say this, make sure that you are authentic in your commitment, and you want to make it happen no matter what it takes.

These sentences mentioned above helps to improve your communication style when speaking to a person or a group of people. They enable you to have a positive outlook and influence on their lives and help build better relationships.

Chapter 14: Strengthening Self-Esteem

***

Why is self-esteem important for entrepreneurs? Once you become an entrepreneur, you have to sell yourself as a brand and product to investors. It comes together. According to Roger Dooley of Neuroscience Marketing, confidence is the most valued element in sales, even more so than competence.

As an entrepreneur, you are continually convincing your clientele that your product or service is needed. To do this without any burnout is to be filled with self-esteem and confidence that you CAN sell your product and service, which is extremely important. In addition to that, you will also be growing your team, and they will require a confident leader. This leadership needs a good dose of self-esteem to build the company and team.

Having self-esteem has little damage to your overall persona. It has less damage than what failure will do to you. As we have mentioned in previous chapters, failure is still an important part of the process of becoming a successful entrepreneur. Combined with self-esteem, it will help push you even when you fail. It will enable you to shake off the dust and get back to the grind. Failure is only failure if you do not continue. But a leader with self-esteem and confidence will learn the lessons taught by failure and keep moving forward.

Many of us think that having self-esteem means we are cocky and arrogant, but this is not true. Self-confident people with self-confidence are usually outgoing and positive. You want to be someone like this, to take you from a good entrepreneur to a better entrepreneur.

Being aware of our emotions means knowing that our feelings can drive our behavior and impact those around us, either positively or negatively. It also means we can manage these emotions, that of our own and that of others, especially at pressuring and stressful times. Self-esteem is a part of our emotions that we can control and determine its effect on people. Self-esteem refers to a person's emotional evaluation of their worth, and this evaluation is based on the beliefs of themselves, their emotional balance, and their various emotional states.

Creating Emotional Balance and Enhancing Self-Esteem

So how do we create emotional balance? Emotional balance is the ability to maintain equilibrium and flexibility between the mind and body when we are faced with changes or challenges. Here are some ways that you can create emotional balance:

1. Accept your emotions

Many of our mental, emotional, and physical problems stem from our inability to express ourselves emotionally. When we are emotional distraught, we smother that feeling in the comforts of eating, sleeping, sweating it out, and sucking it up. It is swept under a rug, we bury it, and project it elsewhere – all in the hopes of suppressing our emotions instead of dealing with it and accepting that this is what we are going through right not. The key here is to allow ourselves unconditional permission to feel – to cry when we want to, to feel anger when we are angry, sadness when we grieve, and so on. Let your guard down, either when you are alone or with someone you trust, and focus on the feeling of your current situation. Experience and immerse yourself in this feeling so you can comprehend better why it hurts and what you will be doing to remedy it once you've accepted and acknowledged your hurt.

2. *Express yourself*

There are many ways to express oneself. Usually, when we experience an angry feeling, we react by crying, shouting, or throwing things. But to identify with ourselves and be able to manage our emotions properly, we can also express ourselves through more positive ways. Some people like reading as it provides an escape into a different world. Some people express themselves through art or music. Whatever it is that you do, make sure you stay connected to discover more about yourself, your identity, and the person you want to become.

3. *Don't hide your feelings*

Sometimes, it is easy to hide our emotions – especially feelings that were the result of painful and scary memories. But as we all know, pushing your memories and feelings aside will only make things worse for you. While it is hard to address your fears, sadness, rage, and anger; once you dive into it, you will find that it will become easier to face your fears and eventually you will become calmer.

Be accepting your past and dealing with it in a more emotional state, you ultimately will lead a harmonious life. Always allow yourself to feel.

4. *See the world in a positive light*

It is easier said than done, we know. Our world is full of hatred, sadness, grief, war, crime, and unfairness – it is a threat to our emotional health. You tend to develop low self-esteem and start asking yourself if you are worth it, can get through it, and if you are doing things right. All these thoughts steer you towards making more mistakes and missteps. Rather than having emotional self-doubt, take action to develop a prerogative of seeing the world in a more positive light.

Do not feel responsible for the bad things that happen –you do not cause them. Have compassion towards yourself and practice mindfulness. Accept that occasional lapses and failures are just part of being human.

5. *Get a grip on your mind*

The way we think causes us emotional distress- this probably is not news to you. We all have this tendency to overthink and think thoughts that do not serve us or give us any positivity. This is just setting you up for emotional distress. So get a grip on your mind and do not let it wander too much.

6. *Practice Yoga and Mindfulness*

Doing yoga daily does help in your mental health- it helps by increasing your confidence in your abilities, and it also helps you make definitive decisions.

You also learn not to be so self-criticizing. Yoga, practiced on a daily basis can help get rid of negative energy within you and help you work your way towards mental clarity and vital energy.

Not only that, the breathing that is practiced in yoga helps you relax and makes you calmer, especially if your mind is racing.

Breathing correctly helps you get rid of stress and anxiety as well.

Chapter 15: Body Language, Your Key to Analyze People

***

Learning to analyze people, their behaviors, and their personalities can be beneficial to you as it can strengthen the relationships you have with them. This relationship can be with anyone whether your partner, your colleagues, your bosses, your family, or even acquaintances. But why analyze people? Firstly, if we could only read people effectively, we would know if they liked something, if they are feeling comfortable, or if they agree to what you say. Secondly, it helps create empathy in you, and when you have empathy you can handle crises and negative situations efficiently. It also enables you to develop better bonds with people.

In a professional capacity, knowing how to read people can take you far up the career ladder, it can help you seal the deal with your business prospects, and it can also create long lasting business relationships. Working on your ability to read and analyze people can significantly effect how you deal with them; this is especially important with people to whom you have a relationship with, whether personally or professionally. When you understand and empathize how someone else is feeling, you can adapt the way you convey your message and communication style so that the person you are communicating with can receive this message in the best possible way.

But how do you analyze people? What signs should you be looking into? What words must you listen to? What other signs can you target to help you understand what someone else is feeling and thinking? When reading or analyzing someone, one of the first few things you must realize is that you need to get rid of your biases and whatever apprehensions you may have made or have on them. These notions are merely walls that contain old and limiting ideas.

How common is body language in communication?

Believe it or not, body language takes up 55% of our daily communication. However, analyzing nonverbal cues isn't focused on just the broad strokes. These gestures indicate various things and depend entirely on context.

Nonverbal cues are incredibly crucial when trying to read someone because, in many ways, you can detect if someone is lying, if they are enjoying a date, or how they are as a person when they come in for a job interview. It is about reading between the lines to interpret body language accurately so that you know if the person's words are conveying how they genuinely feel.

Unfortunately, we humans are more inclined to lie than to tell the truth for plenty of reasons, such as avoiding conflict, trying to impress someone, and so on. Sometimes, we end up lying more than once in a short period, and while they may necessarily not be big lies, we end up doing it anyway. We willingly partake in deception because we would instead tell a sweet lie than the bitter truth. But body language is not as deceptive as words- the human body is a terrible liar.

Body Language Basics

Your main goal when it comes to reading body language is to determine if a person is comfortable in the situation that they are currently in. Once you have established this, the next thing is to process the context that they are in and look at other cues. Of course, this is easier said than done so we will go into the specifics in the following chapters. Here are some common denominators for positive body language:

- Moving or leaning closer to you.

- Feeling at ease.

- Relaxed, uncrossed limbs.

- Long periods of eye contact.

- Looking down and away out of shyness.

- Genuine smiles.

Here are some common denominators for negative body language:

- Moving or leaning away from you.

- The feeling of unease.

- Crossed arms or legs.

- Looking away to the side.

- Feet pointed away from you, or towards and exit.

- Rubbing/scratching their nose, eyes, or the back of their neck.

One body cue can mean plenty of different things. While crossed arms can be construed as negative body language, it can also suggest that that person is feeling cold, uncomfortable, frustrated, closed off, or they may even be more comfortable sitting that way. When reading someone, it is crucial to pay attention to several behavioral cues because looking at one can be misleading. You need to look deeper to understand what is going on, and this means focusing on signals and also the context they are in.

What about the eyes?

The eyes are the windows to our soul. Don't you agree? When we see a person for the first time, our gaze automatically goes to their eyes, looking, searching, and wondering who this person is. We look at the eyes to find out a lot of things about a person from trustworthiness, sincerity, lies, and comfort.

When studying a person by looking in their eyes, try and be subtle and do so without staring into their eyes. You need to maintain eye contact in a friendly manner, and when you have established this, look into the changes in the pupil size. In looking for clues in the eyes of a person, the first step is to know what that person is thinking and to look deeply in their eyes.

What can the eyes tell you?

Apart from the processing of crude information, our eyes can also send more sensitive signals that other people can pick up, especially if they are extremely intuitive. A study conducted by David Lee began by showing participants images of other people's eyes, and he asked them to determine what kind of emotions this person was experiencing. This researcher from the University of Colorado found that participants could correctly gauge the emotions, whether it was anger, fear, or sadness, just by looking at the eyes.

Reveal a truth or a lie

Bet you're thinking of that series 'Lie to Me' in which Dr. Cal Lightman goes through facial cues to determine if a person is lying. The eyes also have the ability to reveal much more complex phenomena, such as whether a person is telling the truth or if they are lying. For example, Andrea Webb conducted a study in 2009, which had one group of participants steal $20 from a secretary's purse, and another control group was asked not to take anything. This research, led by Webb and her colleagues from the University of Utah, showed that pupil dilation gave away the thief. All participants were asked to deny the theft, and the analysis of pupil dilation showed that participants who lied had pupils that were one larger by one millimeter compared to the pupils of participants who did not steal.

Reveals whether a person likes or dislikes something

Our eyes also can become a good indicator of what people like. To learn to read the signs, you would need to look at the size of the pupil as well as the direction of gaze. Take, for example, someone choosing what they would like to eat at a restaurant. We are visual creatures anyway, so our eyes are most likely darting between choosing the salad or the cheeseburger.

Reveals decision making

The other point to look into is decision making. When we are making a difficult decision, our eyes tend to switch back and forth between the different options in front of us and our gaze ends at the option that we have chosen. By observing these little details of where someone is looking, we can identify which options they choose.

Another way of studying this type of difficult trade-off is by offering monetary bets to participants. A study conducted at Brown

University by James Cavanagh had participants that were asked questions involving difficult trade-offs between probabilities and payoffs.

Participants were paid based on their decisions. The researchers found that the harder the decisions were, the more the pupils of the participants dilated. As the choices get harder, our pupils also get bigger.

Reveals if something is unpleasant

The eyes also give away clues to if we experienced something unpleasant. Another study on eyes and their reaction was conducted at the University of Washington in 1999. A painful simulation was administered to the fingers of 20 participants, and they were asked to rate this pain from tolerable to intolerable. The more intolerable the circumstances were, the larger the pupils of the participants became.

5 Ways to Rock Body Language as an Entrepreneur

#1 *Your elevator pitch*

Whether it is pitching to a panel of investors or selling your business idea, the very act of pitching can cause many entrepreneurs, seasoned or new, a little nerves, and you do not want to show that you are worried. When you pitch an idea, you need both verbal and non-verbal communication. Mehrabian, a researcher found that 55% of our usual communication is through non-verbal cues. So what should you be working on when you pitch?

What you say is important but you also want to focus on how you say it. You want to convey strength, confidence and of course humility, based on the facts that you are talking about. Using your hand gestures effectively here will help the people listening to you to remember and understand your pitch.

#2 *Hiring people*

Part of being an entrepreneur is also about finding the right kind of people to work with you. As you continue building your business, you need to develop your team as well and the best way to get the right people is to get your interviewee to speak as much as they can, and as honestly as possible.

One of the ways to do this is to use angled seating. How you sit affects your connection with the candidate. Seating directly results in a lower recall of information, and the person is perceived as being more antagonistic. Seating at an angle is less threatening and encourages a higher bond. Pay attention to any nervous tics you see whenever an important issue is brought up, such as past working experiences, salary, or even family.

#3 Negotiating

Non-verbal behavior has the power to change your feelings of confidence and power, as well as change people's perception of how powerful and confident you are. Before you go into a negotiation, you need to prep not only your points of an argument but also your body language to showcase your feeling of control.

Standing straight showcases that you feel confident. Steepling (when you bring your hands towards your chest or face and press the tips of your fingers together) shows self-assuredness and even superiority. When sitting, do not slouch. Apart from choosing seats at an angle, you should also avoid sitting on low chairs and slouch because this shows that you are small and weak.

Sitting with your arms extremely close or even hugging your body makes you look childlike and weak.

You want to be assertive without being a threat. Sitting tall, nodding your head, looking intently are all facial cues that will help compliment the words that are coming out of your mouth.

#4 Managing

Managing your business, team, and stakeholders expectations are part of the entrepreneurial job scope. You want to be approachable, and you also want your team to be comfortable with you. At the same time, they need to know that you're in control. It is a lot to think about, but here are some body language ideas you can always portray at different points. These are often smiling, leaning towards someone when they speak to you, loosening your shoulders and arms. These are some ways that can show people that they can be open to you.

Being an entrepreneur is a full-time job and juggling both verbal and non-verbal when trying to communicate can be a little hard. With practice and even by watching videos and movies, you can learn how to position your words as well as your body to convey your ideas, your needs, and your expectations without causing miscommunication or conflict.

#5 Networking

Your main goal with networking is to make powerful first impressions because it results in secure connections. So how can you rock your first impressions when it comes to networking? One of the things you can immediately do is to point your feet towards the person you are speaking to. This is an easy way to show that you are engaged in what they are saying, and while it is a simple move, our brain registers this subconsciously as a positive message of staying connected.

One of the worst things you can do is to look past them when talking. Your overhead gaze shows that you are not focused on what they say, so avoid this. According to Dale Carnegie, famous for his self-development and public speaking courses, one right way to make a quick positive impression is by doing the triple nod. It shows people that you are interested in what they are saying and enables them to open up to you more. Three quick nods is a non-verbal language of saying 'Tell me more' or 'I hear you.' You get them to be interested and engaged.

Chapter 16: Cultivating Emotional Intelligence

***

Emotional intelligence is a highly valuable asset. It is the ability to manage and to identify the emotions that belong to you and the emotions that belong to others.

Emotional intelligence encompasses three skills, which are:

1. Emotional awareness.

2. The ability to capitalize emotions and use them on certain tasks such as problem-solving and thinking.

3. The ability to manage emotions which involves regulating personal emotions, cheering people up or calming them down.

The term Emotional Intelligence often referred to as EQ or EI, was coined by researchers Peter Salavoy and John Mayer and later on popularized by *Dan Goleman* in his book with the same name in 1996. With emotional intelligence, you can:

• Recognize, understand and manage your emotions.

• Recognize, understand and influence other people's emotions.

Being aware of these abilities means knowing that your emotions can drive behavior and impact those around you, either positively or negatively. It also means you have the ability to manage these emotions, that of your own and that of others, especially at pressuring and stressful times.

The Five Categories of Emotional Intelligence (EQ)

When it comes to Emotional Intelligence, there are five categories that become a focus.

1. Self-awareness

Having self-awareness means having the ability to recognize an emotion and knowing when it occurs. It is the key to your EQ. To develop self-awareness, a person needs to tune into their own true feelings, evaluating them, and subsequently managing them.

In self-awareness, the essential elements are:

- Recognizing our own emotions and its effects.

- Having a level of confidence and sureness of your capabilities and your self-worth.

2. Self-regulation

When we experience emotions, we often have little control over our actions when we first feel them. One thing we can control, however, is how long these emotions last. To control how long certain emotions last, especially negative ones, specific methods are used to lessen the effects, such as anxiety, anger, and even depression. These methods include reinventing a scenario more positively, through taking a long walk, saying a prayer, and even meditating. Self-regulation includes:

- Innovation - which means open to new ideas.

- Adaptability - to handle change and be flexible.

- Trustworthiness - referring to the ability to keep to standards of integrity and honesty.

- Taking responsibility - conscientiousness of our own actions.

- Self-control - to prevent disruptive impulses.

3. Motivation

Having motivation is what keeps us going to accomplish our tasks and goals and to maintain an air of positivity. With practice and with effort, we can all program our minds to be more positive, although as human beings, it is also good to be negative at times. This does not mean having negative thoughts are bad, but these thoughts need to be kept in check as they cause more harm than good. Whenever you feel like you have negative feelings, you can also reprogram them to be more positive or at least to pick out the positive aspects of the situation, the silver lining which will help you be more focused in solving the problem.

Motivation is made up of:

- Having a sense of achievement and drive to strive to improve and meet a level of excellence constantly.

- Committing to align your individual, group or organizational goals.

- Having the initiative to act on available opportunities.

- Having the optimism to pursue your goals persistently and

objectively, despite the setbacks and obstacles.

4. Empathy

Empathy is the ability to recognize how people would feel towards a particular scenario, thing, or person. Having this ability is crucial to success both in a career and in life. The more you can decipher the feelings of people, the better you can manage the thoughts and approaches you send them. Empathetic people are excellent at:

- Recognizing, anticipating, and meeting a person's needs.

- Developing the needs of other people and bolstering their abilities.

- Taking advantage of diversity by cultivating opportunities among different people.

- Developing political awareness by understanding the current emotional state of people and fostering powerful relationships.

- Focusing on identifying feelings and wants of other people.

5. Social skills

Developing good interpersonal skills is imperative if you want a successful life and a career. In our world today, when plenty of things are digitized, social skills seem to be an afterthought. People skills are more relevant and sought-after then before, especially since now you also need a high EQ to understand, negotiate, and empathize with others. Especially if you deal and interact with different people on a daily basis. Among the most useful skills are:

- Influence to effectively wield persuasive tactics.

- Communication to send out clear and concise messages .

- Leadership to inspire and guide people and groups.

- Change catalyst in kick-starting and managing change.

- Managing conflicting situations which include the ability to negotiate, understand, and resolve disagreements.

- To bond and nurture meaningful and instrumental relationships.

- Teamwork, cooperation, and collaboration in meeting shared goals.

- Creating a synergetic group to work towards collective goals.

Which element is more critical for an Entrepreneur- High IQ or High EQ?

The first question to ask is, what is success as an entrepreneur to you? Is it having loads of money? It is about having a successful career? Is it about having a family? In life, how well you do it depends not only on emotional intelligence but also intelligence, as wel as a little bit of luck and passion. EQ alone is not enough, and neither is IQ. Psychologies agree that among the elements of success is having an IQ count at roughly 10% being the minimum and 25% at its best. The other elements of success depend on everything else, which includes EQ.

It's just like exercise. Working out five days a week alone is not enough. A proper diet, motivation to work out regularly, and making exercise a lifestyle and not an option, are among the traits to achieve a successful and healthy body weight.

10 Qualities of Entrepreneurs with High Emotional Intelligence

There are different types of intelligence, and as life goes on and the world keeps evolving, we discover what these bits of intelligence are and how we can integrate them into our lives. Quotients are what is used to measure the different types of intelligence. While most people are aware of IQ and EQ, there are still plenty of quotients out there that need to be identified such as CQ or curiosity quotient, which focuses on a person's ability to have a powerful motivation to master a specific subject. With the intelligence quotient, or IQ, it is focused on a person's capacity to retrieve and memorize what they have come to know from logical reasoning and memory.

Emotional quotient is the ability to recognize, manage, and understand emotions, that of our own and others. We human beings are emotional creatures who very often respond and make decisions based on our feelings. The need to improve our EQ impacts how our relationships progress and grow, as well as affect the choices we make or even to identify the opportunities that come to us.

In life, having EQ is extremely important, and in this chapter, we will look into the values of having EQ as well as how it can be developed to influence your mind, the minds of the people around you as well as grow emotionally in everything that you do.

1. *People with high EQ have Empathy*

A person with a good sense of empathy can understand, feel, and relate to what another person is going through from within their frame, similarly like walking in their shoes. Having empathy is also a capacity to place yourself in that person's position. Empathy is divided into two types, which are cognitive empathy and affective empathy.

Affective empathy concerns the feelings and the sensations we feel in response to a person's emotions. These sensations are such as mirroring what another person feels, or even the feeling of stress when another person feels anxiety or fear. With regards to cognitive empathy, also known as perspective thinking, it focuses on a person's capacity to understand and identify what someone else is going through emotionally and how they feel.

To have high EQ is to empathize based on other's reactions. Empathy is not something that we are born with; rather it is something that is learnt and cultivated based on the experiences in life. In order to increase your range of empathy, you need to associate your feelings with memories and also the kind of reactions that you want to create out of these memories. The best way is to write these memories down, how you felt, and then also think about how best you could react in these situations.

2. *People with high EQ have Self-Awareness*

The art of self-awareness is understanding ourselves and also recognizing what factors you face and preparing how to manage reactively and proactively. Self-awareness is about how we perceive ourselves and also how we perceive the people around us to see us. An external aspect of self-awareness is the most difficult one to assess properly. A person can learn to see themselves with more clarity by asking what instead of why from critics, seek out honest feedback, and focus on building both internal and external self-awareness. The rewards of self-knowledge are abundant. You can also ask yourself the subjective question, seek out knowledge, and always stay curious.

3. *People with high EQ have Curiosity*

People who are curious, willing to learn, and willing to improve, meet the criteria needed to become successful. Curiosity to learn leads to passion for being the best, and when a person is passionate, they are much more likely to be driven and become better versions of themselves. People who have curiosity never stop learning - they are always in search of things that make them grow and learn. This learning mindset is what you need if you want to increase your emotional intelligence. Wanting to learn and grow is a positive aspect in anyone's life as it helps in both work and relationships.

4. People with high EQ have an Analytical Mind

Emotionally intelligent people are also deep-thinkers, always analyzing and processing the information that they come into contact with. Old habits are also analyzed with old data and the ways of doing things. This is done by the high EQ person to see if these old ways and old information can be improved and made better. In one way or another, each of us is an analysts because we all analyze the kind of information that comes our way.

he thing about people with high EQ is that they become problem solvers and everyday philosophers who always question the WHY and the WHAT. They care passionately about living a virtuous life, which is why plenty of people with high EQ also refer to Stoicism to understand the balance of emotions and rational thoughts in life.

5. People with high EQ cultivate strong Belief

Those with high EQ also place high importance in the power of faith. The power of faith concerns the belief in your capabilities and yourself - that you undertake both in the present and the future. Strong belief also involves believing the path of life is in the experiences, the circumstances, the things and the people that enter our lives. They believe that things happen for a reason and that everything that happens will work out for the best.

Of course, faith alone will not help. Action is also required. Faith, together with hard work, perseverance, and positivity forms the foundations of success in life, at work as well as in relationships. A leader who has a high EQ is someone who uses faith in the emotional, spiritual, and practical context. Meditation is the key to cultivate a firm belief, as it can help you think about how you perceive yourself and the strengths that you have to believe in your capacity and knowledge.

6. *People with high EQ know their Needs and Wants*

The capacity to identify what our needs and wants are is a trait many want but fail to cultivate. People with high EQ, on the other hand, can discern needs from wants. A need, according to Abraham Maslow's Hierarchy of Needs, is our basic necessities - the kinds of things that we need to survive and be safe. When these things are met, everything else is considered a want.

Modern 'wants' are usually a nicer house, a bigger car, better electronics, more comfort, and so on. We do not need these things to survive but we want these things to fuel our personal desires. Knowing what you really need to live, support yourself, and your loved ones, and accomplishing your goals is what ultimately matters. You need to make a clear separation between what is needed and what is wanted.

7. *People with high EQ are also extremely Passionate*

Passion is cultivated from our love to do the things we do. People with a high EQ often use their passion and purpose to spark change, do what needs to be done, and also affect the people around them. This passion is contagious and infectious; it extends to all areas of a person's life, and it also rubs off on those you interact with. Passion is something felt, and when you experience it, you know what you love.

Passion creates drive, ambition, and desire that motivates someone or something. It is what brings out the positive energy that sustains us, even when the going gets tough, and inspires us to keep finding better solutions. It is no secret that people with high EQ are passionate, and they are always persevering and pushing forward despite the circumstances.

8. People with high EQ are Optimistic

Maintaining a positive attitude helps increase the possibilities of getting better opportunities, improving your relationships, and thinking clearly and constructively. Our attitude is always the kind of thing that is within our power to control, not so much the situation or how other people think and act. The choice is ours to live each day with positivity. It's that simple.

9. People with high EQ are easily Adaptable

Adaptability is a crucial trait to have, especially in this day and age. The ability to adapt is the ability to recognize when to continue staying on your course of passion and work and when to change directions. Adaptability is the skill of making crips and quick decisions that creates the best impact in your life.

When a particular strategy is not working, you evaluate and determine what went wrong and create a different approach that will work. Always stay open-minded and be willing to adapt to situations, not only in the way you act and treat yourself but also how you treat the people around you and how to conduct your daily routine. You must also be open to introducing new elements in what you do and how you think. In life, we need to change courses for it to work for our best interests and along the way, make necessary assessments on whether these changes can make you happier and successful. You must realize that change is always possible. There is still the opportunity to start over. It may not be the wisest decision or the more prudent, but you will know in your heart what is or what is wrong.

10. *Success, not only for yourself, but for the people around you*

The need to not only succeed for yourself but also for the people that you are responsible for or work with, is a trait often seen in people with high EQ. This is why they are excellent leaders too. Combined with their passion, leadership, and their optimism, they can drive themselves and the people around them to do what is best. We are often too self-absorbed and concerned with only 'what's in it for me?' This is a good concern to have, so don't be convinced that this is not right. But while looking out for ourselves, we also need to maintain a spirit of hope and desire to see the people around us succeed.

This type of thinking and way of life safeguards you against greed and envy, and it also revitalizes both our passion and our drive to achieve our next goal. We also become better at gaining allies and build substantial and meaningful relationships that will ultimately help us when reaching our goals.

Benefits of Emotional Intelligence

Physical Health

Your physical health is vital to our wellbeing. It is all about taking care of your body and managing stress levels so that your physical wellbeing can correlate with our emotional wellbeing. Having a good state of emotional intelligence and physical health helps us all to maintain a healthy lifestyle.

Mental Well-Being

Apart from physical wellbeing, emotional intelligence has a direct correlation to your attitude and outlook on life. A good balance of EQ can help lighten anxiety and prevent mood swings and depression. It makes us more positive, and we look at life with a happier outlook.

Relationships

When we understand and manage our emotions, we are better equipped at communicating our feelings in a clear and constructive way. This also helps us relate to people who are in a relationship with us. We are better at understanding their needs, feelings, and responses, and they, in turn, can better understand us. This leads to a stronger and meaningful relationship.

Conflict Resolution

Having a good dose of EQ also means that it will be much easier to resolve conflicts or even avoid them before they begin. This is because you would be able to discern people's emotions and empathize with them. Because we can understand the needs and desires of others, we are also better at negotiating to bring out the best resolution that is mutually beneficial for both parties. It is easier to give people what they need and want if we can understand where they are coming from.

Success

We also develop stronger internal motivators when we have better EQ. This means we procrastinate less, we have more self-confidence, and we become much better in focusing on our tasks. Along the way, we also create better networks of support and persevere with more resilience to overcome setbacks and move on. We look at the long-term benefits and see how it affects the success rate.

Leadership

People with higher EQ are better leaders simply because they have a better ability to comprehend what motivates people, can relate to issues and tasks in a positive manner, and can also build stronger bonds with people in the workplace. A capable leader can identify the needs of the people in their team or company and also see how these needs can be met in a way that can encourage better performance and increase workplace satisfaction.

Leaders that are savvy and emotionally intelligent build stronger teams because they focus on utilizing the emotional diversity of their team members. While more research needs to be done to understand emotional intelligence, the basic understanding is that emotions affect the overall quality of both our personal and professional lives and it plays a more crucial role than that of brain intelligence.

It is never too late to learn to master a good sense of EQ. When you continuously learn and adapt to your situation and empathize with people, it will not only make it easier for you to cultivate better relationships but also make your life happier.

What can you do to increase your emotional intelligence as an Entrepreneur?

1. Observe your feelings

One of the first things we lose touch with is our emotions, especially when we focus all our energy into worrying about what to do next and what can be done better. Instead of focusing on our feelings, we instead choose to ignore them quite often. Things become worse when we start suppressing our feelings instead of dealing with them. When we keep covering up our emotions, we tend to lose control of them, and that is not a good thing.

When we experience an emotional reaction towards something, it is almost always because we have unresolved issues. The next time you feel like a negative emotion is taking up space in your mind and heart, take a 5-minute breather, calm down and think about what you are experiencing and also the possible reasons that culminate these emotions. Write things down and try to identify your triggers and how you can deal with them.

2. Practice responding, not reacting

When we react, often we do it unconsciously to relieve the emotions that we are experiencing or express what is going through our mind. When we respond consciously, we are more adept at paying attention to our own feelings, and we also become better at deciding how we will behave in reaction to these emotions at that time. As we become more aware of our emotional triggers, we become more aware of how to adapt, how to respond, and how to behave.

For instance, if you know you get angry quickly and you have a habit of throwing a temper tantrum when things get stressful, relive this moment when you are alone and think about how and what you would have preferred to do for the next time, to prevent yourself from experiencing the same trigger. Speak to your colleagues and tell them you need some time-out to gather your thoughts. Leave the room if you must, go out and get some fresh air – Count to ten even. Once you have calmed down a little, you will be better at dealing with the issues you face, that made you angry in the first place.

3. *Stay humble all the times*

Staying humble enables you to make better and meaningful relationships. When you presume that you are better than other people, it becomes harder to see your faults, and you will get emotional easily over things that do not meet your expectations or needs.

To prevent this, you can start looking at things from a different perspective. Put yourself in the person's shoes and understand how they feel or how they would think of a certain situation. Doing so would make you more prone to understanding people's thoughts and feelings even more. You will also learn a thing or two about how to deal with similar situations. Being humble is knowing that you are not any better than anyone else and also wise enough to know that you are special in your own way.

Chapter 17: Dealing with Insecurity

When someone is behaving irrationally, you have to remind yourself that this could be because they are acting out of a certain emotion. It also could be that their insecurity is behind this false sense of bravado. When you notice this, you will more likely procure a sense of empathy for these people who act arrogantly or rudely because what they are trying to do is cover their insecurity.

What about you, as an entrepreneur? It is not wrong to feel insecurity at times. After all, we often have to speak in front of an audience or present to people who have much more experience than us or have more knowledge about something.

More often than not, this insecurity stems from other people's reaction towards us. Because they feel insecure, they hide it by putting us down, and that's not good. Nobody has the right to make you feel inferior.

This insecurity can be about anything – looks, power, money, smartness. Most of these insecurities creep out from a sense of material value. Sometimes insecurity can be justified, but most of the time, it is not. Insecurity manifests differently, and it can range from the inability to accept that you've done a great job, accept a compliment, or even not wanting to wear a swimsuit to the beach.

None of these traits help us to behave virtuously. There is a fine line between being insecure and being a brat. Here are some identifying factors that can help you separate the good and the bad:

1. Self-kindness is not Self-Judgement

Compassion towards someone who is insecure is being understanding and warm to them when they fail, or when they suffer, or at moments when they feel inadequate. We should not be ignoring these emotions or criticizing. People who have compassion understand that being human comes with its own imperfections and failing is part of the human experience. There will inevitably be a failure when we attempt something because failure is part of learning and progress. We will look into how failure is a friend in disguise in the next chapter. Having compassion is also being gentle with yourself when faced with painful experiences rather than getting angry at everything and anything that falls short of your goals and ideals.

Things cannot be exactly the way they should be or how we dream them to be. There will be changes, and when we accept this with kindness and sympathy and understanding, we experience greater emotional equanimity.

2. Common humanity and not Isolation

It is a common human emotion to feel frustrated, especially when things do not go the way we envision them to be. When this happens, frustration is usually accompanied by irrational isolation, making us feel and think that we are the only person on earth going through this or making dumb mistakes like this. News flash- all humans suffer, all of us go through different kinds of suffering at varying degrees. Compassion involves recognizing that we all suffer and all of us have personal inadequacies. It does not happen to 'Me' or 'I' alone.

3. *Mindfulness is not Over-Identification*

Compassion needs us to be balanced with our approach so that our negative emotions are neither exaggerated nor suppressed. This balancing act comes out from the process of relating our personal experiences with that of the suffering of others. This puts the situation we are going through into a broader perspective.

We need to keep mindful awareness so that we can observe our negative thoughts and emotions with clarity and openness. Having a mindful approach is non-judgemental, and it is a state of mindful reception that enables us to observe our feelings and thoughts without denying them or suppressing them. There is no way that we can ignore our pain and feel compassion at the same time. By having mindfulness, we also prevent the over-identification of our thoughts and feelings.

Discovering Compassion

You're so dumb! You don't belong here, loser! Those jeans make you look like a fat cow! You can't sit with us! It's safe to say we've all heard some kind rude, unwanted comments either directly or indirectly aimed at us. Would you talk like this to a friend? Again, the answer is a big NO.

Believe it or not, it is a lot easier and natural for us to be kind and friendly to people than to be mean and rude to them whether it is a stranger or someone we care about in our lives. When someone we care for is hurt or is going through a rough time, we console them and say it is ok to fail. We support them when they feel bad about themselves, and we comfort them to make them feel better or give a shoulder to cry on.

We are all good at being understanding and compassionate and kind to others. How often do we offer this same kindness and compassion to ourselves? Research on self-compassion shows that those who are compassionate are less likely to be anxious, depressed or stressed and are more resilient, happy, and optimistic. In other words, they have better mental health.

Identifying someone with Insecurity and how to Deal with it

Based on what was discussed above, when we can identify when a person is acting out of insecurity, it can enable us to protect ourselves from engaging in a mindless power play and feel insecure ourselves. People who are insecure tend to spread their negativity and self-doubt to others as well and here is how you can identify them and decide whether to show compassion or to show them the exit:

#1 People who are insecure try to make you feel insecure yourself

You start questioning your own ability and self-worth. This happens when you are around a specific person. This individual has the ability to manipulate you and talk about their strength, and try to put you down. They project their insecurities on you.

#2 Insecure people need to showcase his or her accomplishments

Inferiority is at the very core of their behavior, and for people like this, compassion is just a waste of your time. They feel insecure, and to hide it, talk about their accomplishments in a way to make others feel less than. They always brag about their fabulous lifestyle, their wonderful shoes, their huge cars, and their elite education. All of this is done to convince themselves that they do have it all and you have nothing.

#3 People who are insecure drops the "humble brag" far too much

The humblebrag is essentially a brag that is disguised as a self-derogatory statement. In this social media age, you can see plenty of humblebrags who complain about their first-world problems such as all the travel they need to do or the amount of time they spend watching their kids play and win games or even the person who complains about having a tiny pimple when the rest of their face looks flawless. Social media is ripe with people who are narcissistic, and this is not worth your time. Do not feel any less just because someone shows off how much traveling they need to do.

#4 People who are insecure frequently complain that things aren't good enough

They like showing off the high standards that they have, and while you may label them as snobs, you know that it is all an act. They proclaim their high standards to assert that they are doing better than everyone else and attempt to make you feel less yourself and more miserable. Pay no attention to people like this.

Conclusion

Thank you for making this sound decision of purchasing this book. We hope that this book has given you a deep wisdom of entrepreneurship that goes beyond finance, management, and business skills. The elements covered in this book can be applied by anyone to level up their skills.

It does make sense that people who have better self-esteem, communication skills, and better sleep, and compassion are better people, which ultimately leads to becoming top-notch entrepreneurs. This is simply because they are happier and optimistic about their future.

We hope this book helps you to revisit other aspects of entrepreneurship because to become the best version of yourself is more than just knowing how to run a business and having a great product. A healthy mind, body, and presence, can make you a more sustainable, productive entrepreneur. It will also stop you from self-sabotage, whenever feelings of insecurity, incompetence, or worthlessness. When our positive inner voice triumphs and plays the role of the supportive friend, we create a sense of safety, and we accept ourselves enough to see a better and clear vision. When we eat better and pay more attention to our body, we have a sharper focus on what our mission is and what goals need to be met. We then work towards making the required changes for us to be healthier and happier.

If you have found this book beneficial and you are happy with what you have gained in reading it, I'll be glad to read your opinion with a brief review on Amazon so that other people will be able to reap the benefits of this book too.

www.ingramcontent.com/pod-product-compliance
Lightning Source LLC
Chambersburg PA
CBHW060904170526
45158CB00001B/486